Mediterranean Soups

The People, Places, and 125 Authentic

Matera, Italy

Mediterranean Soups

Best-Loved Soup Recipes

Text and Illustrations by
Carol Robertson

Photographs by
David Robertson

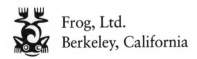
Frog, Ltd.
Berkeley, California

Published by Frog, Ltd.

Frog, Ltd. books are distributed by
North Atlantic Books
P.O. Box 12327
Berkeley, California 94712

Interior photos by David Robertson
Cover photo by Brooke Warner
Cover and book design by Paula Morrison

Printed in the United States of America

Library of Congress Cataloging-in-Publication Data
  Robertson, Carol, 1942–
    Mediterranean Soups / by Carol Robertson.
      p.   cm
    Includes index.
    ISBN 1-58394-044-8 (alk. paper)
    1. Soups.   2. Cookery, Mediterranean   I. Title.
  TX757.R625   2001
  641.8'13—dc21
                                                      00-060996

1 2 3 4 5 6 7 8 9 / 05 04 03 02 01

"Soup puts the heart at ease,
 calms the violence of hunger,
 and eliminates the tension of the day."
—Escoffier, 1847–1935

Church, southern France

This book is dedicated to my grandmother Carolina Stiffa, a true Mediterranean spirit, and to my husband David who has "adopted" a love of all things Mediterranean. Both, in their own ways, have taught me to appreciate and honor my heritage.

Special thanks to the many friends and relatives, both here and abroad, who have contributed family recipes. Thanks, too, to my husband for his help and patience.

Table of Contents

· ·

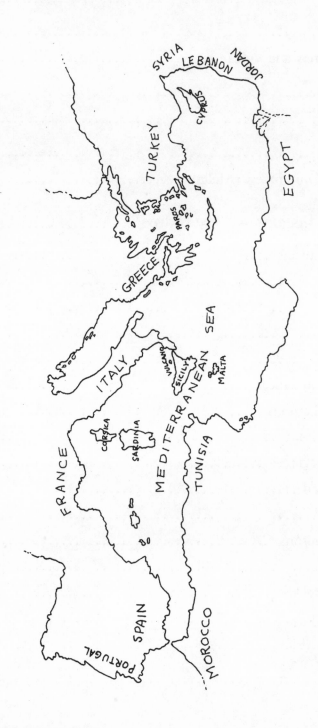

The Mediterranean

· ·

The Mediterranean is the cultural focus in many of our lives. The people of the Middle East, North Africa, Europe, and in large measure those of North and South America are people of this "middle land." A cauldron of cultural development, homeland to three major religions—Islam, Christianity, and Judaism—and seat of Greek, Arabic, and Roman language and culture, the Mediterranean means home to a large percentage of the world's people.

It is possible on a map to draw a wide circle around the Mediterranean—ancient people did just that and knew very little of other lands—to see what, 2,000 years ago, was essentially an inland sea for the exchange of ideas, art and artifacts, people, and of course, foods. One can see how this sea became geographically and culturally central to the inhabitants of lands as diverse as hot, dry, coastal North Africa and the pine-covered forests of Greece and Spain.

From the beginning of recorded time Mediterranean people have been connected to their land; the land and sea themselves have been the bonds that contain the diversity.

Is there something about the light, the strong sun in a cloudless sky, the abundance of healthy food, and the relatively safe and placid sea that helps make the cultures of Spain, Portugal, southern France, Italy, Greece, Turkey, the Middle East, and North Africa so special? Time after time, since our first visits to these lands many years ago, we have returned to learn and understand more about these people who are "us." What is this seductive draw? Is it the light, is it the people, is it the food, is it the history?

For me, the Mediterranean holds a great sense of place—my grandmother was born in Sorrento, near Naples in 1891, coming

· ·

Children dressed for a festival, Spain

here with her parents as a young child. My grandfather came here alone, as a teenager from a small town in Calabria, in Italy's "toe." The household they eventually created together formed many of my early memories and impressions. The foods they ate, watching them as they tended their chickens and vegetable garden, the relatives who were always around; it's easy to understand how I came to love the Mediterranean culture.

Luckily, my husband, who is half Irish and half Scot, is equally enamored with and fascinated by all things Mediterranean. He first traveled there long before we met, and speaks constantly of impressions gathered from visits to Sicily, parts of North Africa, Lebanon, and some Greek islands. It has been my good fortune that he, too, has been imbued with a love of the area. We together have visited and revisited the many countries and three continents that surround, what in Arabic translates to, "the white sea in the middle." Each time, we enrich ourselves by reconnecting to people, places, history, and food.

The sunny Mediterranean spirit, and the robust, hospitable nature of the people, come across in their remarkable cuisines. Each is different, but their link is the use of foods in a straightforward and unmannered way. There are no fussy sauces or complicated procedures; the dishes are as honest as their ingredients.

Olive oil is at the top. Its golden richness is pressed from the olives growing on the uncounted millions of trees that are everywhere. It is this nutritious oil, along with garlic, tomatoes, onions, eggplant, fennel, lemons, grapes, basil, mint, rosemary, coriander, lentils and beans, pine nuts and almonds, cumin, cinnamon, honey, and seafood of all kinds that form the backbone of the healthy Mediterranean diet.

Cuisines evolve, usually from generations of home cooks using the ingredients at hand to feed their families. In a Mediterranean climate of hot, dry summers and cool, rainy winters, with every country touching the sea, it is not surprising that seafood, grains and beans, "summer" vegetables of all kinds, field herbs and greens, nuts and olives, cheese from the milk of small animals, delicious fruits from trees and vines, and spices brought overland from the East, began to combine into the diverse, yet connected, cuisines that today circle the Mediterranean.

Mediterranean Soups

· ·

With the exception of perhaps a piece of meat thrown on a campfire thousands of years ago, it is easy to believe that soups were man's first cooked foods. His earliest containers were filled with water, then bits of meat or fish, field greens, herbs, grains, beans, and vegetables. Left to cook for hours, soups in their thousands of incarnations were born.

Everywhere in the world, cooks discovered the particular magic of soup. In this most frugal and nutritious of preparations, nothing is lost. The soup pot accepts it all; the bit of meat clinging to the bone, scraps of vegetables, salt, a rind of cheese or heel of bread, all are transformed by the alchemy of heat and time. From these humble beginnings, housewives have ingeniously created soups that have become fixed in the repertoire of a region's cuisine.

Almost anything that tastes good on its own will taste good incorporated into a soup. It can be simple or complex, long simmered, quick cooked, or not cooked at all. It can be delicate or robust, hot or cold. It is a symbol of hospitality and brings people together. Who can eat a big, hot, bowl of soup without stopping to sit? It warms on a cold day, and cools on a hot one. It is the first dish—sometimes the only dish—of a meal. Soups are very forgiving of the novice cook, and can be made ahead—indeed are often improved by the wait.

The soups chosen for inclusion here are the most traditional. Look elsewhere for fancy adaptations, fussy preparations, esoteric ingredients, and "fusion" recipes.

In every case, we present recipes that are straightforward, honest, and authentic. Our travels leave us with vivid memories of wonderful soups eaten in the homes of friends and relatives, and in

· ·

restaurants throughout the Mediterranean. From among the thousands of possibilities we have chosen the ones we loved best.

Soups are virtually always served with the bread of the area; flatbreads in North Africa and the Middle East, or thick slices from the fat, crusty loaves of the western Mediterranean. Of course, fresh ingredients are key. Use of seasonal products has always been associated with careful cooks, and is synonymous with good eating. Each season has its food—a tradition that is still very much alive throughout the Mediterranean. We, in the United States, would do well to return to these ideas in an age when virtually no one grows or gathers his own food. Peaches, cherries, and fresh baby field greens are available all year. While we shouldn't shun the products we can enjoy in this age of fast global transport, there will always be something sensually rewarding in the wait and anticipation of eating the first spring asparagus—in the spring!

What makes a soup Mediterranean? Typically, Mediterranean soups begin with aromatic vegetables such as garlic, onions, carrots, and celery, plus herbs and spices, being gently cooked in olive oil. Stock or water and salt are added, and then grains, beans, pastas, vegetables, and perhaps bits of meat or fish; the quickest cooking items last. Each country, each region, each cook has her variations. There are the classics: minestrone in Italy, bouillabaisse in southern France, caldeirada in Portugal, harira in Morocco, and gazpacho in Spain.

In addition, there are soups made without garlic or even olive oil—the yogurt soups of Turkey, and the creamy lemon-egg soups of Greece. Some soups are served cold but most are served hot. Many have a traditional flourish added at the last moment; garlicky rouille in France, harissa in Morocco, peppery butter in Turkey. What they do have in common are fresh ingredients, robust flavors, frugality, and nutrition, plus a directness and sense of hospitality that comes straight from the people of the Mediterranean.

Ingredients

• There are some recipes for homemade chicken, beef, lamb, and fish stock in the last section of this book. Homemade is the most economical, if not the easiest way to go. All stocks freeze well. You can save up meaty bones and other ingredients in a freezer bag (frozen) until you are ready to make stock. However, in all recipes calling for stock, it is fine to substitute good quality canned stock in equal measure for homemade.

• The one exception to the "never used canned vegetables" rule, is in the case of canned tomatoes—you are better off using canned, rather than the half-ripe tomatoes that are too often found in supermarkets. Only use fresh tomatoes if you can get fully ripe ones in summer.

• Always use extra virgin olive oil in all recipes calling for olive oil. If you can buy large bottles of it, keep it refrigerated. It will turn rancid if left for any time on a shelf. Do not be concerned with it turning cloudy and thick. A short time at room temperature returns it to a clear green-gold liquid.

• Use fresh herbs such as rosemary, cilantro, parsley, thyme, sage, and basil. Try growing small pots of each. They freeze well if wrapped tightly. To use in soups, quickly unwrap, snip off directly into the soup, rewrap and return to the freezer. (Don't try to use frozen herbs in salads, though—they will look black).

- Always use fresh garlic. Do not substitute powdered, or the already-diced variety soaking in oil.

- The only place in this book that contains a few unusual items is in the Middle Eastern Soups section. It is well worth your time to go to a Middle Eastern specialty grocer for items such as kiskh, pomegranate syrup, and bulgur. They will refrigerate or freeze well, and repay you with authentic taste.

- "Pepper" in the recipes refers to coarsely ground fresh black peppercorns.

- Lots of finished soups freeze well, but we like to make just enough soup to last for two meals or one big party. Some ingredients, like root vegetables, become watery upon defrosting, and pastas become overcooked and broken with reheating. Egg and cream soups may separate. Experiment; it might be just as easy to make and freeze stock only, completing the soup when you plan to serve it.

Restaurant, Portugal

The Soups of
Portugal and Spain

Of all the cuisines of the European Mediterranean (southern Italian, French, Portuguese, and Spanish), the everyday foods of Spain are the most hearty, even heavy. Portions are enormous, and while the Italian cuisine relies on vegetables, Spanish dishes are full of meat and eggs. With the exception of the many varieties of gazpacho, soups are stew-like, with assortments of meats and sausages, seafoods, chicken, and beans predominating.

The soups of Portugal tend to be somewhat lighter, as is the rest of their cuisine. However, their seafood chowders are justifiably famous—big filling soups brimming with shellfish, squid, garlic, tomatoes, and bread.

There is always a danger in characterizing any culture in a few words or phrases. All of its people are, of course, not alike, but in our stays in Iberia, both in Portugal and Spain, we think we have uncovered the subtle markers that define cultural differences.

We found the people of Spain to be reserved and thoughtful, but unfailingly polite and friendly to outsiders. Lurking there is the faintest hint of sadness. Farmers, shopkeepers, restaurateurs, and housewives alike quietly go about their responsibilities. Living in what is often a difficult landscape, and traditionally kept to strictly conservative ways by church, state, and family, people from the highest to the lowest exude a calm, and are patient and enduring. Even their day, with its long siesta period, has a stately and measured quality to it. To an outsider it seems to go on forever, from early morning into the even earlier morning hours of the next day. Little children are out and about, or still sitting at dinner at midnight, in a day broken by a long afternoon nap. We had often commented that we received two days for the price of one while traveling in Spain.

Sharing the Iberian Peninsula with Spain is Portugal. The Portuguese are more open and ready to smilingly engage the stranger. It may be that centuries of seafaring exploration, and, indeed, the tiny size of their country, which makes virtually everyone an outsider, contribute to this sunny quality. In this country-in-miniature, one finds harsh mountains, magnificent vistas, and cozy semi-tropical beaches. The Portuguese are hard working, traditionally as fishermen and vintners, farmers, and crafts people.

The Iberian Peninsula was occupied by the Romans as one of their most prized territories. It was they who introduced wine, cured meat, and olive oil. They built roads, cities, temples, aqueducts, and theaters, and it is from Latin that all the western Mediterranean languages spring.

Hundreds of years later, about 700 A.D., the Muslims arrived carrying their architecture, knowledge of science and art, and food items like rice, oranges, lemons, almonds, and exotic spices such as cumin, cinnamon, saffron, and nutmeg.

Seven hundred years later, in the 15th century, New World foods such as tomatoes, potatoes, squash, beans, peppers, and corn found their way to Portugal and Spain. Today, soups from both countries display these cultural markers.

Although the Spanish eat their soups to start a meal, their most complex would make a complete meal for us. The same applies to the fish stews of Portugal. But the lighter soups are wonderful for lunch, and as a first course at dinner. Spanish families begin to eat dinner at about nine o'clock, but in Portugal, dinner is served in both homes and restaurants starting around seven o'clock.

Portuguese Soups

Lisbon, Portugal's capital, is a lovely city for walking and exploring. It is small as main cities go—all the better to enjoy its charms. Its fine waterfront on the Tagus River has been a seaport for 3,000 years. The Phoenicians, Greeks, Romans, and Muslims all left their mark, and it was central to Portugal's growth as a 15th-century maritime power.

History aside, we found it to be a welcoming, flower-filled city of broad avenues, fine shops, wonderful museums, and a bustling waterfront. Fascinating, too, was a ride to the top, and a long walk down from, Lisbon's highest point. Crowned by the medieval castle of St. George and the Al Fama district, Lisbon's oldest quarter, its narrow streets are made for strolling. The whitewashed houses crowd the cobblestone lanes. Ground-floor dwellings open into restaurants. Many are decorated in typical Portuguese fashion, with blue and white tiles.

It was in one of these restaurants that we ate a particularly delicious *caldeirada*—a classic Portuguese fish soup. The heavy scent of garlic, olive oil, and tomatoes in a rich broth drifted up from two steaming bowls. We ate every bit, and sopped up every drop with crusty Portuguese bread.

Portuguese Fish Soup (Caldeirada)

 4 tablespoons olive oil
 1 large onion, chopped
 1 green pepper, seeded and chopped
 2 cloves garlic, minced
 1 cup dry white wine
 1 14-ounce can diced tomatoes
 1 bay leaf
 3 cups chicken stock
 1/2 teaspoon hot red pepper flakes
 1 1/2 pounds mixed fish fillets such as cod, haddock, snapper, etc., cut into 1 1/2-inch cubes
 2 dozen cherrystone clams in their shells
 1 loaf crusty French bread
 1/2 cup fresh cilantro, chopped

In a large saucepan, heat the oil and slightly brown the onion. Add the pepper and garlic, and sauté for another minute.

Add the wine, and boil and reduce over high heat for 3 minutes. Add the tomatoes and their liquid, the bay leaf, stock, and hot pepper.

Simmer for 15 minutes. Add the fish pieces and cook for 5 minutes. Add the clams and cook for 5 minutes longer.

In the meantime, cut a thick slice of bread per person, and place one in the bottom of each broad soup bowl. Ladle the broth, fish, and clams over the bread. Garnish with chopped cilantro. Serve with additional bread.

Serves 4.

One evening in Lisbon we decided to visit a fado club. They are restaurants that feature guitar players and singers who specialize in performing that most typical of Portuguese music, the sad and haunting songs called *fado*. Most are located in either the Al Fama or Barrio Alto districts, old quarters on two of the seven hills on which Lisbon is built.

We asked the proprietor of our small hotel for a recommendation and took a taxi to the Barrio Alto. We entered a charming and intimate wood-paneled restaurant with a tiny stage. We enjoyed our dinner, which started with a chicken, lemon, and mint soup, and as we were finishing, a man with a guitar quietly seated himself on a stool on the stage. A woman, dressed in a simple dress and black shawl, walked over to stand beside him. He played one or two chords, the room grew still, and with eyes closed, the woman began to sing. Her voice was low but strong. Although we could not understand the words, for an hour we sat there totally absorbed in listening to soulful songs of lost loves, the pull of fate, and the tragedies of life.

Chicken and Rice Soup with Mint

> 1 1/2 quarts chicken stock
> 1 onion, finely chopped
> 1/3 cup uncooked rice
> 1 whole chicken breast
>   juice of one half lemon (about 2 tablespoons)
> 1/4 cup fresh mint, minced
>   salt and pepper to taste
>   lemon slices

Pour the stock into a large saucepan. Add the onion, rice, and chicken breast. Simmer for 30 minutes and remove the chicken.

Pull the chicken off the bone and cut into strips. Return it to the stock, along with the lemon juice.

Add the mint, salt, and pepper to the stock. Simmer several minutes to heat through.

Serve garnished with thin lemon slices and additional mint leaves. Serves 6.

The Monument to the Discoveries, Lisbon, Portugal

Lisbon's waterfront, along the Tagus River, has been in use for 3,000 years. One day we took a taxi to its farthest point, intending to walk back, stopping at sights along the way. Our first stop was Belem Tower, a severe-looking, five-story, gray stone building constructed in 1515. It is a proud reminder of the days when it was used as a lookout for the returning ships of the explorers.

Across the avenue and a short walk away is the enormous and ornate Hieronymite Monastery. It was built in the Manueline style with riches pouring in from the New World. Attached to it is the Maritime Museum, which houses the ships that carried brave explorers to unknown lands. Back across the wide avenue and on the edge of the river stands the Monument to the Discoveries, built in 1960 to honor Prince Henry the Navigator, who, it can be said, pushed Portugal to prominence 500 years ago. It was he who encouraged the exploration of unknown destinations.

After a long day of visiting the four sites, we finally stopped at a restaurant to eat. We ordered a seafood soup that was pure Portuguese, and seemed so right to eat in the spot along the waterway that made its history possible. This soup was an açorda, that is, a soup which always uses bread slices or breadcrumbs to add thickness and body.

Shellfish Açorda

   2 dozen cherrystone clams
   3 cups day-old French bread
1/2 cup olive oil
   3 garlic cloves, minced
   4 cups chicken stock
1/3 cup chopped parsley
     salt and pepper to taste
1/2 pound small raw peeled shrimp
   4 eggs
     lemon wedges for garnish

Steam the clams in a large covered pot until they just open. Remove them from their shells, and discard any that do not open. Set aside.

Cut the crust off and crumble 3 cups of bread. Heat the olive oil in a large skillet, then cook the garlic until golden. Then remove it from the oil and save. Add the bread. Toss it until coated with the oil. Fry until it is crisp. Add back the fried garlic bits. Set aside.

In a deep saucepan, heat the chicken stock, and add the parsley, salt, and pepper. Add the shrimp and clams to the stock. Gently break the eggs on top of the simmering stock. Cover and simmer very gently for about 5 minutes, or until the shrimp are pink and the eggs are just set.

Lift the eggs to a dish, and divide the stock and shellfish evenly into 4 soup bowls. Divide the fried breadcrumbs over the fish in each bowl. Top each portion with a poached egg.

Serve at once with lemon wedges.

Serves 4.

Soups using fish are predictably common throughout the Mediterranean. The variations are endless, with every country having its favored ingredients. This version comes from the recipe collection of Rosella Lopes of Stonington, Connecticut, a town that still has a sizable Portuguese community. The thousand-year-old influence of the Muslims can still be tasted in the pinch of saffron.

Rosella's Fish Chowder

> 1 tablespoon olive oil
> 1 large onion, chopped
> 1 14-ounce can diced tomatoes
> 1 teaspoon salt
> 3 small potatoes, peeled and cut into cubes
> 4 cups water or chicken stock
> 2 pounds fresh codfish cut into 1-inch cubes
> 1 tablespoon vinegar
> 1/4 teaspoon saffron threads

In a large saucepan, heat the oil and add the onion. Brown slightly, and add tomatoes, salt, potatoes, and water or stock. Simmer for 20 minutes.

Add the fish, vinegar, and saffron. Simmer for an additional 10 minutes, or until the fish and potatoes are cooked.

Serves 6.

Soon after arriving in Portugal for our first visit, we drove north out of Lisbon to the old fishing village of Nazaré. We planned to stay for a few days and soak up what everyone assured us was a piece of old, coastal Portugal. This was many years ago and I'm not sure that Nazaré remains just this way today, but then it was a revelation.

Nazaré is really two towns; the lower town, Praia, or "beach," is the fishing village, which was already full of tourists enjoying its fine beach. We preferred to walk the steep and quiet side streets where the families of the fishermen lived. At the time we were there, the people still wore traditional clothing. The women were barefoot with short, many-layered skirts. The men, in plaid shirts and long pants, had long black stocking caps on their heads. Racks of fish were drying in the sun and salty air.

The second town, Sitio, is high on the sheer cliff behind the town. Its women were dressed in long black dresses and shawls that protected against the constant whipping winds of their high village. The views up and down the coast from this site were spectacular.

I'm not sure if this was the first time we ate this soup in Portugal. It certainly was not the last, as every restaurant and every housewife prepares it constantly. The shredded kale it calls for is sold by

Drying fish. Nazaré, Portugal.

the kilo, and it is traditionally served with corn bread. Seated at a tiny restaurant in high Sitio, with views that went on forever, the taste of this soup came to mean Portugal to us.

Potato and Kale Soup

> 1/3 cup olive oil
> 1 medium onion, chopped
> 1/4 pound garlicky smoked sausage such as chorizo, sliced
> 3 medium potatoes
> 6 cups water
> 1/2 pound kale
> salt to taste

Heat the oil in a skillet. Sauté the onion and sliced sausage. Set aside.

Peel and dice the potatoes, and cook them in the water until quite soft. Mash them into the water.

Slice the kale leaves as thinly as possible into fine julienne shreds. Add to the potato water. Simmer for 10 minutes, then add the reserved sausage, onion, and oil. Heat through for 1 or 2 minutes. Add salt to taste.

Serve immediately with lots of bread.

Serves 4.

In the far south of Portugal is a region known as the Algarve. It is tiny, perhaps twenty by eighty miles. It is warm virtually all year, with the first almond blossoms appearing in January and February. The Greeks, Phoenicians, Romans, and Muslims have all left their mark in the architecture and foods of the area. Its southern edge is lined with beautiful and dramatic beaches. We enjoyed several days there one year, at the beaches and buying pottery in the small inland towns.

The restaurants away from the tourist areas are wonderfully friendly, and encouraged us to come into the kitchens to make our selections. In one kitchen we found a line of hinged copper vessels on a long fireplace. Several cooks were tending them, and the waiter encouraged us to select one for our dinner. Not quite sure what would arrive, we returned to the dining room. Several minutes later our "cataplana" arrived. The hinged lid was removed to reveal a dozen steamed clams in a tomato-based broth that contained cubed pork. This soup, plus lots of the wonderful yeasty and crusty Portuguese bread, made a memorable meal. We have since eaten the unusual pork and clam combination elsewhere in Portugal, but never again in its traditional cataplana.

Pork and Clams in a "Cataplana"

1/2 cup olive oil
  2 pounds lean pork, cut into 1-inch cubes
  1 pound linguica or chourico sausage, crumbled or diced
1/4 pound prosciutto or cured ham, diced
  3 medium onions, chopped
  4 cloves garlic, minced
  3 bay leaves
  2 teaspoons sweet paprika
  1 cup fresh parsley, chopped
  1 teaspoon hot red pepper flakes
3/4 cup dry white wine
  1 14-ounce can diced tomatoes
  3 cups chicken stock
  3 dozen fresh clams

In a large deep skillet with a tight fitting lid, heat the oil and brown the cubed pork, then the sausage, then the prosciutto. Add the onion and garlic and brown 2 minutes more.

Add the bay leaves, paprika, parsley, hot pepper, and wine. Cook on high until the wine has lost its alcohol and reduced by half, then add the can of tomatoes with its liquid.

Add the chicken stock. Cover and cook on simmer for about 45 minutes or until the pork cubes are tender. This can be made up to a day ahead to this point.

Just before serving, place the clams, hinged side down, on top of the meat mix, cover tightly, bring to high heat, and cook without opening for 10 minutes. Discard any clams that do not open.

Serves 6.

We ate a soup similar to this—there are hundreds of variations—at a restaurant in the Algarve region in the south of Portugal. The broth is often served as a separate soup, but the soup itself is really a complete main dish. This version belonged to Rosella Lopes, who was born nearly 100 years ago on Sao Miquel in the Azores, and enjoyed a reputation as a fine cook in the Portuguese community of Stonington, Connecticut.

Cozida

> 1 cup dried chickpeas, soaked overnight in cold water
> 1 bone-in smoked pork shoulder
> 1 pound linguica or chourico, crumbled
> 4 medium potatoes, peeled and cut into large sections
> 1/2 cup split peas
> 1 can fava beans, drained
> 1/2 pound kale, chopped (or cabbage cut in wedges)
> 1 cup elbow macaroni
>   salt and pepper to taste

Drain the chickpeas and set aside. In a large pot, cover the pork shoulder with water. Bring to a boil. Skim off the foam as it rises to the surface. Lower the heat and simmer for 2 hours.

Remove the shoulder from the pot, and when it is cool enough to handle, cut off about 1 pound of meat. Reserve the bone for another use and add the meat to its broth in the pot.

Add the chickpeas and all other ingredients, except the macaroni, salt, and pepper to the broth. Simmer, covered, for several hours more, stirring occasionally and adding more water as necessary.

Add the macaroni for the last 15 minutes. Add salt and pepper to taste.

Serves 6.

Whenever we are in Portugal or Spain we make a point of staying at a few of the extraordinary, government-run Portuguese *pousadas* or Spanich *paradors*. The government has rescued old castles, monasteries, and mansions from ruin, and, with a sure eye, has restored them into first-class hotels and restaurants. Each is a showcase for local arts, crafts, antiques, architecture, and food. Over the years, we have visited many—sometimes just for a meal, but more often to stay the night. All of the fine foods featured in their dining rooms are specialties of that region.

One of the most dramatic and beautiful is the Pousada da Rainha Santa Isabel in Estremoz, Portugal. It is housed in a castle that sits high on a hill. We could see it from miles away and drove higher and higher until the road at last ended in a huge courtyard surrounded by a wall and watchtowers. While several small boys practiced soccer there, we admired the view of the windswept valley below.

Great wooden doors opened into the soaring lobby of the 13th-century castle. From there we were led to our antique-filled room. Out the open window we could see and hear hundreds of swallows as they dipped and swooped by.

Later that night we began our dinner with this soup, a specialty of the pousada. Açordas are Portuguese soups that always include bread. They are thick and hardy, a meal in themselves.

Tomato Açorda

  3 cloves garlic, minced
  1 onion, chopped
  1/3 cup olive oil
  2 14-ounce cans diced tomatoes
  1 tablespoon fresh oregano *or* 1 teaspoon dried oregano
  2 bay leaves
  1/4 cup chopped parsley
  6 cups beef stock
    salt and pepper to taste
  1 loaf crusty French bread
  1 egg per serving

In a large saucepan, brown the garlic and onion lightly in the olive oil. Add the tomatoes, oregano, bay leaves, and parsley. Simmer for 10 minutes.

Add the beef stock, and simmer, covered, for 1 hour. Stir occasionally. Add salt and pepper to taste.

Before serving, cut 1 thick slice of bread per serving, and place in the bottom of each soup bowl.

Gently break the eggs into the simmering soup to poach for 5 minutes. Spoon some soup, and 1 egg, over the bread in each bowl. Serve with additional bread.

Serves 6.

Europe's westernmost point lies on the coast of Portugal at a place called Cabo da Roca. We drove there from Lisbon one day, parked the car, and slowly walked the path to the edge of a sheer cliff overlooking the sea. We were the only people there. The view was exhilarating and terrifying at the same time. The calls of hundreds of seagulls flying far below carried up to our ears, over the sound of the pounding surf. The wind tore at our clothes as we stood looking out over the vast Atlantic Ocean, trying to imagine how the early Portuguese explorers must have felt. We were impressed with their courage.

After leaving the cape we drove inland to the little village of Colares, known for its red wines, and ate a late lunch of this tomato and sausage soup. If the best vine-ripened tomatoes are not available, canned tomatoes make a fine substitute. Plan to serve it with lots of bread. The Portuguese way is to place the bread in the bottom of each bowl and pour the hot soup over it.

Tomato and Sausage Soup

    2 tablespoons olive oil
  1/2 pound chourico sausage, sliced
    2 medium onions, sliced
    1 14-ounce can diced tomatoes, *or* 1 pound of fresh tomatoes
    5 cups chicken stock
    1 bay leaf
  1/2 cup chopped parsley
      salt to taste
    1 small red or green chili pepper, chopped

In a saucepan, heat the oil. Brown the sausage and onions in the oil until the onions are golden. If you are using fresh tomatoes, peel, seed, and chop them before adding them to the sausage and onions. If you are using canned tomatoes, pour them, with their liquid, into the pot with the sausage.

After cooking them for 5 minutes, add the stock, bay leaf, parsley, salt, and chopped chili. Simmer gently for 30 minutes. Serve with or over bread.

Serves 4.

The fortified town of Obidos, about sixty miles north of Lisbon, can be seen from many miles away. It sits on a hill surrounded by a calm lagoon. All of the buildings are tucked within the completely surrounding crenellated walls. Visitors must leave vehicles outside and enter through a serpentine gate under a watchtower.

This we did one day, stepping back a thousand years. Built by the Muslims and won back by the Portuguese in the 12th century, the town became the traditional wedding gift of each succeeding king to his queen.

It is quite small—one main street with a few cross streets and narrow lanes. The houses and shops are white, with windows and doorframes painted in clear reds, blues, and yellows in the Portuguese manner. Flowers cascade from balconies. The main road leads straight to the Moorish castle at the highest point in town. It has been converted into an inn *(pousada),* and the majestic dining room serves regional food. We stayed for lunch that began with small bowls of this unusual soup. Tripe is esteemed on the Iberian peninsula, and it is well worth the effort to prepare this delicious soup. Make ahead to allow the flavors to blend.

Tripe Soup

    1 pound precooked tripe, cut in 1 inch squares
    1 meaty veal shank
   1/4 cup olive oil
   1/4 pound prosciutto or other cured ham, chopped
   1/2 pound chourico sausage, sliced
    2 medium onions, chopped
    3 carrots, peeled and sliced
    1 cloves garlic, minced
   1/2 small chicken, cut into 5 or 6 pieces
1 1/2 quarts chicken stock
   1/2 teaspoon ground cumin
   1/2 teaspoon hot red pepper flakes
    1 bay leaf
   1/4 cup chopped parsley
      salt to taste
    1 14-ounce can navy or other white beans

Place tripe and veal in a large soup pot, cover with salted water, and simmer for 50 minutes, or until the tripe and veal are tender. Remove from the water, and when cool, pick the meat off the veal shank. Put both the veal and tripe aside.

Wash and dry the pot, and heat the oil in it. Sauté the prosciutto, chourico, onions, carrots, garlic, and chicken pieces for 10 minutes.

Pour in the chicken stock, cumin, pepper, bay leaf, parsley, and salt. Add the reserved veal and tripe. Simmer covered for 20 minutes, or until all the meats are tender.

Add the drained beans and cook for an additional 10 minutes.

Serves 6.

Spanish Soups

The hot, dry climate of Andalusia, in southern Spain, gave birth to the cold refreshing soups known collectively as gazpachos. We think of gazpacho as a tomato-based "salad in a blender," but actually tomatoes were not used widely in southern Europe until several hundred years ago. The original concept was introduced by the Romans as a cold bread, garlic, olive oil, and water soup. Later the Muslims added nuts, hot pepper, cumin, and fruit to their versions. Until recently it was thought of as a cold lunch for peasants toiling in the fields.

We enjoyed both of the following versions in the charming city of Seville. If you ever go there, try to stay in the beautiful Santa Cruz district. It is close to everything and has many tiny streets of white houses and shops, wrought iron balconies covered with flowers, and colorful tiles set into the walls. Blessedly, there are no cars allowed!

Classic Andalusian Red Gazpacho

    2 14-ounce cans diced tomatoes
1 1/2 cups peeled cucumber pieces
    1 green pepper, cored, seeded, and cut into pieces
    1 clove garlic, sliced
    1 small onion, chopped
    2 tablespoons red wine vinegar
    4 tablespoons olive oil
  1/2 teaspoon salt
  1/2 teaspoon freshly ground black pepper
    1 slice of bread, crusts removed, soaked in water

Suggested garnishes:
- finely diced cucumbers, onions, peppers, and tomatoes
- chopped parsley
- hard boiled eggs, diced
- garlic croutons, page 253

Place all the ingredients, except the garnishes, in a blender or food processor. Work in batches if necessary, and blend until a smooth purée is formed. Adjust the amounts of vinegar and salt to taste. Add ice water if the soup is too thick. Chill thoroughly for several hours. Add more water if needed.

Prepare the garnishes. Present the ice-cold bowls of soup accompanied by small bowls of any or all garnishes.

Serves 6.

Note: Also see Almond Soup—really another gazpacho.

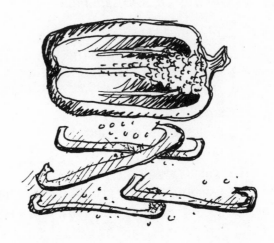

Like classic red gazpacho, this spicy white gazpacho is also typical of Andalusia. Such light, cooling vegetable soups are seldom found in northern Spain, with its harsh winter climate.

Gazpacho Blanco

      3 cucumbers, peeled, seeded, and chopped
    1/2 small onion, chopped
      1 clove garlic, chopped
      1 bell pepper, cored, seeded, and chopped
    1/2 teaspoon cumin
      1 tablespoon lime juice
    1/2 teaspoon Tabasco sauce (or more to taste)
      3 cups buttermilk, sour cream, or yogurt
         salt to taste
    1/2 cup finely minced cilantro *or* parsley

Suggested garnishes:
    - finely chopped scallions, chives, cucumber, green pepper
    - sliced toasted almonds
    - sliced green grapes

Place all the ingredients, except the cilantro or parsley and garnishes, in a blender or food processor, and purée. Taste for additional salt, Tabasco, or lime juice. Add cilantro or parsley. Add water if soup is too thick. Mix well. Refrigerate for several hours until thoroughly chilled.

Present with small bowls of any or all garnishes.

Serves 4.

Andalusia, the whole of southern Spain, is perhaps the most romantic of all the provinces. It is a true Mediterranean area—sunny, hot, and full of white-washed villages, great castles, and stately cathedrals. It is worth a visit there if only to see the wonders of Seville, Granada, and Cordoba. To us it is the true Spain, with its flamenco dancers and matadors. In Andalusia, so close to Morocco, Muslim influence lingers longest and is felt most keenly. The architecture, and especially the food, hearken back to pre-15th century Moorish Spain.

Foods such as saffron, almonds, cumin, cinnamon, nutmeg, oranges, and lemons are still central to the cuisine. This almond soup is very ancient. It is quite rich, simple, and delicious. Like red and white gazpacho, it is also a gazpacho.

Almond Soup (Ajo Blanco)

>   4 thick pieces country-style white bread with crusts cut
>   off—about 1/2 pound
>   1 tablespoon vinegar
>   1 cup almonds
> 3 to 4 cloves garlic, chopped
>   1/2 cup olive oil
>   1 quart cold water
>   salt to taste
>   white grapes *or* peeled, cubed apple (optional)

Soak the bread in water and then squeeze it dry. Add the vinegar and mix it in.

If the almonds still have their brown skins, place them in boiling water for 1 minute. Then pop them out of their skins with your fingers.

Place the almonds, garlic, and oil in a blender or food processor. Grind the almonds as fine as possible. Add the bread and half the water, continuing to blend. It should be smooth and creamy with no graininess from the almonds.

Strain into a bowl if there are any almond pieces, then add the remaining water. Add salt and stir to blend. Refrigerate for several hours.

Serve with some grapes or small cubes of peeled apple mixed in, if desired.

Serves 4 to 6.

The ancient walled city of Avila lies about seventy miles west of Madrid. It is completely enclosed by miles of watchtowers and battlements, and its walls are among the best preserved in all of medieval Europe. They were completed in the 11th century and remain intact today. To visit Avila on its high elevated plain is to step back in history.

In the 16th century a Catholic mystic—the nun who would be canonized as St. Theresa—lived here, and she is still strongly associated with the city. We drove to Avila to see her convent, the walls, and the city's numerous churches. We stayed at another of the government paradors, this one reconstructed to resemble an old inn. The dining room served a savory garlic soup as part of a three-course dinner. Spanish olive oil is more strongly flavored than Italian, and Spaniards like their garlic slightly browned to heighten its flavor. Thus, this recipe is typical of Spanish soups.

Garlic Soup

> 1 entire head of garlic, separated into cloves and peeled
> 4 tablespoons olive oil
> 4 thick slices crusty country-style bread
> 1 teaspoon sweet paprika
>   salt to taste
> 1 quart water
> 4 eggs

Mince 2 cloves of the garlic into 2 of the tablespoons of olive oil in a small pot. Heat until the garlic begins to color. Remove from the heat and brush this garlic-scented oil onto both sides of the bread. Place the bread under a hot broiler until it toasts; turn and toast the other side. Set aside.

In a soup pot, place the other 2 tablespoons of oil, and lightly brown all of the other whole cloves. Add the paprika, salt, and water. Bring to a boil, reduce to a simmer, cover, and cook for 30 minutes.

Mash the softened garlic into the water, or purée in a blender.

Heat the oven to 350°. Put 1 piece of toasted bread into the bottom of each of 4 ovenproof soup bowls. Divide and ladle the soup over the bread. Carefully break 1 egg into each bowl, over the hot soup and bread.

Place the bowls in the hot oven for 5 minutes or until the eggs are half set. Serve immediately.

Serves 4.

Tomatoes are a New World import to Europe, only dating from the exploration of the Americas in the 15th century. For a Johnny-come-lately, they have taken the Mediterranean by storm, and have, as we all know, become inextricably linked with southern European cuisines.

Tomato-based fish stews such as this are common along the coasts of Spain and Portugal, wherever housewives have a handful of assorted fresh fish caught by their husbands and a handful of their own garden vegetables. All of these vegetables grow especially well in the hot, dry climate of the Mediterranean summer. The saffron, cumin, and orange are Moorish influences.

Spanish-Style Mixed Fish Stew

          6 tablespoons olive oil
          1 onion, chopped
          2 cloves garlic, chopped
          1 14-ounce can diced tomatoes
        1/2 cup chopped parsley
        1/2 teaspoon saffron threads
          1 teaspoon cumin
          1 tablespoon fresh grated orange rind—just the orange
            part, not the white
          1 quart chicken stock *or* water
        18 small clams and/or mussels, cleaned
          4 squid, cleaned (see note), and sliced into 1/2-inch rings
          1 pound assorted white fish, cut into 1-inch cubes
            salt and pepper to taste
          6 thick slices crusty country-style bread
          2 whole cloves garlic

In a deep pot, heat 4 of the tablespoons of oil, and sauté the onion and garlic for 3 minutes. Add the tomatoes, parsley, saffron, cumin, and orange rind. Simmer, covered, for 15 minutes.

Pour in the chicken stock and bring to a boil. Lower to a simmer. Add the clams. Bring back to a simmer. After 3 minutes, add the squid and fish. Cook all for no more than 4 minutes more, or until the clams are open. (Discard any that do not open.) Gently stir with a wooden spoon once or twice. Add salt and pepper to taste.

In the meantime brush the bread on both sides with the remaining 2 tablespoons of oil. Toast each side under a broiler, and then rub both sides with a garlic clove.

Place 1 piece of bread in each of 6 soup bowls, and divide the seafood among the bowls. Discard any clams that did not open. Ladle the tomato broth over all.

Serves 6.

Note: To clean squid; cut off the head, and pull the contents, including the hard quill, out of the body cavity. Pull off the thin membrane that covers the body. You will now have a clean white tube. For this recipe, slice it into 1/2-inch rings.

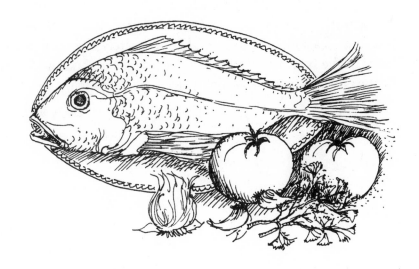

Years ago, when our two daughters were eight and nine years old, we traveled with them from the lush vineyards of southern France, across the rocky snowfields of the Pyrenees, and into the arid hills of northern Spain, to visit Olite, with its parador (inn). The governments of Spain and Portugal have rescued crumbling castles, monasteries, and mansions of historical significance and turned them into first-class hotels full of antiques and regional foods. We have never been disappointed with our stays in them.

We drove over winding empty roads and through old villages to the 12th-century castle of Olite. Our room there was in the tower, with its own circular stone staircase. Our girls were thrilled to be staying in a "real castle," and played for hours on its great stone staircases.

The next day we drove east toward Barcelona, to another parador in Cardona. We could see the 8th-century mountaintop monastery and church from many miles away. That night we dined on regional specialties in the great vaulted hall of the monastery. Here we tasted this salt cod soup. The next day we toured the severe and majestic 8th-century church whose lowest foundations had been laid in 400 A.D.

In Spain and Portugal, coastal towns enjoy fresh fish and shellfish, but inland, traditionally the only fish has been salt cod. Over the centuries this cheap, non-perishable fish has been relied on by peasants as a source of protein. Unfortunately, the great cod-fishing areas of the North Atlantic have been depleted, and the former fare of the poor has become a high-priced specialty item.

Salt Cod Soup (Bacalao)

> 1 pound salt cod, soaked in water for 24 hours, with the
>   water changed 3 times
> 1 small hot chili pepper
> 2 tablespoons olive oil
> 1 onion, chopped
> 2 cloves garlic, minced
> 1 14-ounce can diced tomatoes
> 2 medium potatoes, peeled and cut into 1/2-inch dice
>   salt to taste

Drain the cod of its last change of salty water. Place in a pot of fresh water to cover, and bring to a boil. Remove from the heat immediately, and let it cool in the water. If the water seems too salty, repeat the boiling step with fresh water.

In the meantime, remove the stem and seeds of the chili and mince.

In a skillet, heat the oil and sauté the onion and garlic for 5 minutes. Add the tomatoes with their liquid, the chili, and the potatoes. Cover and simmer for 10 minutes.

Remove the cod and measure its cooking water. Pull apart the cod, looking for any bones. Put the shreds and pieces of cod back in the pot, along with about 3 cups of its water.

Add the cooked tomatoes and potatoes, then bring to a simmer for 5 minutes. Add salt to taste. Serve with Italian bread.

Serves 4.

Madrid is not our favorite European capital. It has been the capital for less than 500 years and is still too "new" for our tastes. It does, however, have the magnificent Prado Museum, lovely parks, and the best bullfight ring in Spain.

One evening in an outdoor restaurant in the Plaza Mayor, we had a typically enormous Spanish meal, which began with this soup, one of the cornerstones, along with gazpacho and cozida, of Spanish soup cuisine.

Galician Soup (Caldo Gallego)

    1 cup dry white navy beans, soaked overnight
    1/2 pound chourico sausage
    1/2 pound smoked thick-cut bacon, cut in a large dice
    2 quarts beef stock
    2 large potatoes, peeled and cubed
    2 turnips, peeled and cubed
    1 onion, chopped
    2 carrots, peeled and sliced
    1/2 head cabbage, cut in large chunks
    2 cups coarsely chopped kale
    6 cloves garlic, cut in half
      salt and pepper to taste
      olive oil

Place the beans, chourico, and bacon in a pot of beef stock. Simmer for 2 hours.

Remove the sausage and slice. Return to the pot and add the potatoes, turnips, onion, carrots, cabbage, kale, garlic, salt, and pepper.

Continue to simmer for 1 hour, or until everything is very tender and the beans are starting to break up. Add water as necessary.

Serve immediately or reheat the next day. Drizzle a bit of olive oil over each bowl.

Serves 6.

The drive north from Morocco to Granada was not an easy one for me. I felt awful. Having just come from North Africa, I realized in hindsight that I had allowed myself to become dehydrated in the hot desert air. When we settled in our hotel, I craved some sweet soft drinks, and then, later, a salty soup.

We found a lovely outdoor restaurant, in a courtyard behind the cathedral and royal chapels, where I had this soup. The next day, when I had recovered, we went to visit Granada's most famous sight, the Alhambra. The builders of this Moorish palace, a last stronghold of the Muslims in hot southern Spain, understood how to use water to cool. Trickling fountains and cascades are everywhere. They made use of mazes and small gullies just beneath the walkways where the sight, and even the sound, of water adds to the refreshing illusion. Each room, courtyard, and garden, spread over many acres, is more beautiful than the next. In the heart of the palace is the Court of Lions, often photographed and probably the most well-known area of the palace.

Ham and Bean Soup with Fresh Herbs

> 1/4 pound thick cut smoked bacon, cut into 1/4-inch dice
> 1 tablespoon olive oil
> 1 onion, chopped
> 2 cloves garlic, minced
> 1/4 pound cured pork (a ham hock or piece of prosciutto)
> 1 14-ounce can diced tomatoes
> 1 quart chicken stock
> pepper to taste
> 1 14-ounce can chickpeas, drained
> 1/2 cup fresh parsley, chopped
> 1/2 cup fresh mint *or* cilantro, chopped

In a deep pot, cook the bacon for 4 minutes. Add the oil and sauté the onion and garlic for 4 minutes.

Add pork, tomatoes, stock, pepper, and chickpeas. Bring to a boil, reduce to a simmer, cover, and cook for 1 hour.

Add the fresh herbs. Cook for 10 minutes more. Allow the soup to rest for 15 minutes.

Serve hot with lots of fresh bread.

Serves 4.

Toledo, the former capital of Spain, is still lovely, sitting as it does on a high hill overlooking a flat plain. It retains much of its early appearance because it depopulated with the rush of citizens to the new capital, Madrid, in the 16th century. It is the city of El Greco, the painter, and a magnificent cathedral and fortress. We drove the fifty miles from Madrid in the late spring, when the weather was still somewhat cool, and spent several hours visiting the main sights.

In mid-afternoon we stopped for lunch in the Barrio Rey or "king's district," in a small restaurant off a cobblestone plaza. In Spain it is easy to be sated with meat, and yearn for vegetables. This is one of the rare soups that is (almost) without meat or fish.

Vegetable Soup with Chickpeas

       2 tablespoons olive oil
       2 cloves garlic, minced
       1 onion, chopped
       2 ounces prosciutto, diced
       1 green bell pepper, seeded and cut into strips
       1 carrot, peeled and cut into thin rounds
       1 potato, peeled and cut into small cubes
       1 cup green beans, cut into 1-inch sections
       1 14-ounce can diced tomatoes
       1 14-ounce can chickpeas, drained
    1/4 cup fresh parsley, chopped
          salt and pepper to taste
       1 teaspoon ground cumin
       1 teaspoon dried oregano
       4 cups chicken stock

In a soup pot, heat the oil and sauté the garlic and onion. Add the prosciutto, pepper, carrot, potato, and beans.

Pour in the tomatoes and chickpeas. Add the parsley, salt, pepper, cumin, and oregano. Pour in the chicken stock.

Bring all to a boil, reduce to a simmer, cover, and cook for 40 minutes. Allow the soup to rest for 15 minutes, then serve it with lots of bread. Serves 6.

City gate, Spain

Spaniards, like all Mediterranean people, love the taste and smell of garlic in their foods. Virtually all their soups contain at least a bit. This one is a chicken vegetable soup, which has its garlic in a mayonnaise that is floated on the top. We ate a soup like this in the extreme south of Spain, near Gibraltar, in a town called Jerez de la Frontera.

Many years ago the English came to that area to establish wineries which, to this day, still produce most of the world's great sherries. Virtually all have English names but are thoroughly Spanish in character. Look at your finest sherry bottle. It will have probably been bottled in Jerez (which means sherry). We toured two of the wineries there and then ate a simple lunch in a restaurant in Jerez's old quarter.

Chicken Vegetable Soup

    1/2 of a small chicken
      1 bulb fennel, cut in 8 pieces
      1 large onion, chopped
    1/2 pound mushrooms, washed and sliced
      1 14-ounce can diced tomatoes
      2 cups packed fresh spinach, chopped
      1 14-ounce can white navy beans, rinsed
    3/4 cup packed basil leaves
  1 1/2 quarts chicken stock
         salt and pepper to taste
    1/2 loaf French bread, cut in thick slices and toasted
      1 recipe garlic mayonnaise (aioli) page 247

Place all the ingredients, except the bread and mayonnaise, in a soup pot. If there is not enough stock, add water to cover everything.

Bring to a boil, reduce to a simmer, cover, and cook for 1 hour.

When this soup has cooled, or the next day, remove the chicken. Take the meat off the bones, chop, and return it to the soup. Discard the bones.

Reheat the soup if necessary, and ladle over toasted bread in individual bowls. Pass the garlic mayonnaise so each can add a tablespoon to their soup.

Serves 6.

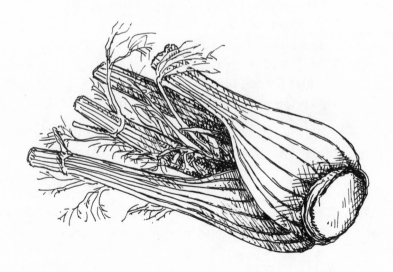

We were driving through central Spain, west of Madrid and headed toward Portugal, when we stopped to look at an old church in a small town. Wandering around looking for the best photo angle, we heard a friendly "hola." An old man seemed to understand our desire and motioned for us to come with him. He led us down a lane and through his garden gate. There, indeed, beyond some fruit trees, was the most interesting view of the church. He then began to show us his chickens and pigs, tomatoes and peppers, fig trees and pears, and all the other crops on his small farm. All the while, his five-year-old grandson followed devotedly, gazing up at him with such admiration that we wished we could have understood more. He explained as well as he could the history of the area and his church.

This area in central Spain can be harsh. Mostly a high arid plain with strong winds and cold winters, it favors hearty food. The *cocido* (like the Portuguese cozida) is a one-dish meal of soup, beans, meats, and vegetables. We have eaten cocido like this several times in central Spain. Plan to take two days to prepare it.

Cocido

> 1 pound fresh beef brisket
> 1 pound mixed cured pork such as prosciutto, ham hocks, or picnic shoulder
> 1 pound veal shoulder
> 2 onions, cut in quarters
> 3 carrots, peeled and cut in 1-inch pieces
> 1 small head cabbage, preferably Savoy
> 1 cup dried chickpeas, soaked overnight
> 2 large potatoes, peeled and cut in quarters
> 1 pound garlicky sausage, such as chourico or kielbasa

Put the beef, pork, and veal in a deep pot. Cover with water and bring to a boil. Reduce to a simmer and cook for 1 hour. Skim off any foam. Add water as needed to keep the meat covered.

Add the onions and carrots. Cut the cabbage into quarters and add it to the pot. Add water to cover if necessary, and simmer for 30 minutes.

Refrigerate overnight. The next day skim off any fat that has congealed on top.

Bring the chickpeas to a boil in their pot. Simmer for 45 minutes. Drain.

Add them, plus the potatoes and sausage to the big pot. Simmer all gently for another 30 minutes. Let the soup rest off the heat for 20 minutes.

Slice the meats and cabbage. Divide and arrange portions of each in deep wide soup bowls, then ladle the broth, beans, and other vegetables over all.

Serves 8.

The Soups of Southern France

. . . .

The French have developed two cuisines. The first was originally created for the nobility and upper classes, and today is found in good French-style restaurants all over the world. The second is the cooking done by home cooks. In the south of France, this home-style cooking, different from that in northern France, is distinctly Mediterranean.

Its roots lie in the earliest influences of the Phoenicians, Greeks, Romans, and later, the Muslims. Two of its principle ingredients, tomatoes and peppers, came from the New World after the 15th century. The food history of the three areas of France rimming the Mediterranean (Languedoc, Provence, and Rousillion) is the same as that of southern Spain and Italy. It is based on the abundance of local vegetables, herbs, seafood, and meats. In comparison to the cuisine of the north, the cooking of the south rarely aspires to more than creating honest and delicious dishes using the materials at hand. Several thousand years of trade, a bold climate, and the needs of fishermen and farmers to feed their families have created what we enjoy today in the foods of southern France.

The soups especially seem to distill the essential ingredients of the land and sea into flavorful and satisfying dishes. A southern French trick with soups is to swirl a rich dollop of spicy, garlicky sauce into individual bowls. *Aioli, rouille,* and *pistou* are names to remember when constructing a true Mediterranean French soup. Most of the soups are vegetable and seafood based, with a few based on meats,

. . . .

herbs, beans, and grain.

From Nice in the east to the Spanish border in the west, southern France is blessed with hot, dry summers and cool, rainy winters. The scent of wild herbs and the sound of cicadas fill the air. Many small fishing villages, with medieval towns perched high in the hills behind them, dot the landscape. To the south lie the azure waters of the Mediterranean.

Sête, France

Nice is a jewel of a city. International travelers have flocked for generations to its pebbly beach, grand hotels, charming villas, and four-star restaurants. Many hotels line the world-famous seaside Promenade des Anglais, where the stately Hotel Negresco is the centerpiece. Ever since our first, separate, visits there—me on post-college budget travel, my husband courtesy of the Navy—we have both always gravitated to the small, family-run, honest restaurants in the warren of streets that is old Nice. They are nothing much to look at, but they specialize in the inexpensive and authentic food of the area. There is *pissaladière* (the pizza of Nice), *socca* (huge pancakes of chickpea flour sold by the piece), and, of course, wonderful bowls of fragrant soups—especially fish soups.

The most famous of all French Mediterranean soups is bouillabaisse. No two cooks make it in exactly the same way. There is a great deal of debate about which varieties of fish to use, whether or not it should contain potatoes, and how it should be served. This soup is an adaptation of a recipe sent to me by Roselyne Melhmann, who lives in Marseilles.

Bouillabaisse

> 4 tablespoons olive oil
> 6 cloves garlic, sliced
> 2 large onions, sliced
> 6 ripe tomatoes, peeled and chopped, *or* 2 14-ounce cans
> diced tomatoes
> salt to taste
> 1/2 teaspoon hot red pepper flakes
> 2 bay leaves
> 4 ounces anise flavored liqueur, such as ouzo or pernod
> 1 tablespoon grated orange rind
> 1/2 teaspoon saffron
> 1 quart fish stock *or* bottled clam broth
> 6 potatoes, peeled and sliced

3 pounds assorted, cleaned, large pieces of fish such as
   snapper, cod, perch, monkfish, or bass
6 slices French bread
1 recipe rouille, page 248

In a large soup pot, heat the oil, and sauté the garlic and onions. Add the tomatoes, salt, pepper, bay leaves, anise liqueur, orange rind, saffron, and stock. Bring to a boil, lower to a simmer, cover, and cook for 30 minutes.

Uncover and add the potatoes. Cook for 10 minutes. Add the fish and cook gently for another 10 to 15 minutes.

In the meantime, toast the bread on both sides under a broiler.

When the fish and potatoes are done, spoon them onto a serving platter. Keep them warm for serving after the broth.

Ladle the broth into 6 soup bowls. Place at least 1 tablespoon rouille on each piece of bread, and float them in the broth. Serve the rest of the rouille in a small side dish to accompany the fish.

Serves 6.

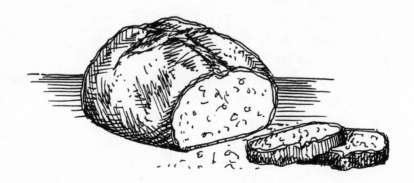

Marseilles is one of the truly ancient ports of the Mediterranean. Its harbor, guarded on both sides by castles, opens its arms to the quais beyond. High on a hill is the cathedral of Notre Dame de la Garde, with the city at its feet. It is a bustling port of pleasure yachts, fishing boats, and ferries leaving for Corsica and points beyond.

One July we were staying with friends just outside the city. At their suggestion, we were excited to be traveling into the port to see the gala fireworks celebrating Bastille Day.

Unfortunately we started out too late, and Damien, our host, was left to search for a parking spot while we were let out to run down a side street to join the crowds at the harbor. The effect of the explosions of color outlining and flood-lighting the ancient fortifications made it all worthwhile. As for our host—*c'est dommage*—perhaps next time.

Bourride à la Marseilles

> 4 tablespoons olive oil
> 1 leek, white part only, washed and sliced
> 2 large onions, sliced
> 4 cloves garlic, minced
> 1 14-ounce can diced tomatoes
> 3 pounds *soup* fish (small whole bony fish, fish heads, bones)
> 2 tablespoons tomato paste
> 1/2 teaspoon saffron
> 2 bay leaves
> 2 sprigs fresh thyme
> 1/2 cup coarsely chopped parsley
>   salt and freshly ground black pepper to taste
> 2 pounds assorted, cleaned, boneless fish pieces, such as snapper, perch, cod, monkfish, or bass
> 1 thick slice French bread per serving
> 1 recipe aioli, page 247

In a large casserole, heat the oil and sauté the leek, onions, and garlic. Add the tomatoes, soup fish, tomato paste, saffron, bay leaves, thyme, parsley, salt, and pepper. Add water to cover. Bring to a boil, reduce to a simmer, cover, and cook for 30 minutes. Cool a bit.

In a fine sieve or strainer, strain off the broth into a soup pot. Push and mash the heads, bones, fish, and vegetables against the strainer to extract as much broth and flavor as possible. Test for salt and pepper. Add water, if necessary, to create a fairly thick soup.

Put the soup back in its pot. Add the 2 pounds of cleaned fish pieces. Bring to a simmer and cook, covered, 10 minutes or until the fish is opaque and flaky.

In a meantime, toast the bread, or sauté it on both sides in additional olive oil. Put one piece in each serving bowl. Remove the fish pieces to a platter and keep them warm.

Swirl about 3 tablespoons of the aioli sauce in the soup. Ladle the soup over the bread pieces.

Serve the soup, along with the platter of fish and the rest of the aioli, which can be put on the fish or into the broth.

Serve it with lots of additional bread and a green salad.

Serves 4 to 6.

Another popular fish soup that we've enjoyed comes from the area around Toulon, a seaport that lies between Marseilles and Nice. It is called Le Revesset and contains greens in the broth.

Toulon Fish Soup

    4 tablespoons olive oil
    1 clove garlic, minced
    2 cups Swiss chard, washed and chopped
    2 cups spinach, washed and chopped
  1/2 cup sorrel, washed and chopped
      salt to taste
  1/4 teaspoon hot red pepper flakes
    2 tablespoons lemon juice (1/2 lemon)
    1 quart fish stock, water, *or* bottled clam broth
    2 pounds assorted, cleaned, boneless, white fish pieces
      such as cod, haddock, snapper, or bass
    4 thick slices French bread
    2 cloves garlic, peeled

In a soup pot, heat 2 tablespoons of the oil, then sauté the garlic for 1 minute. Add in the greens, stir to wilt, cover, and simmer in their own juice for several minutes.

Add the salt, pepper, lemon, and stock. Bring it to a boil, reduce to a simmer, cover, and cook for 10 minutes. Add the fish pieces, cover, and cook gently until they are opaque and flaky (about 10 minutes).

In the meantime, brush each side of the bread with the remaining 2 tablespoons of oil. Broil under a hot broiler until browned, then rub each side with the peeled garlic cloves.

Place 1 piece of bread in each bowl. Pick the fish out of the soup to serve separately on a platter. Spoon the broth and greens over the bread.

Serves 4.

One of the most lovely soups of the south of France is a creamy mussel soup with an infusion of saffron. We ate this as a first course in a "fancy" restaurant near the Spanish border.

Creamy Mussel Soup from Sête

    1 recipe aioli, page 247
    2 tablespoons olive oil
    2 cloves garlic, minced
    2/3 cup white wine
    3 tablespoons fresh parsley, minced
    1/4 teaspoon saffron
    2 dozen mussels, cleaned
    1 cup heavy cream
      salt and freshly ground black pepper to taste

Prepare the aioli. Place in a small bowl to be served with this soup.

In a lidded soup pot, heat the oil, sauté the garlic for 2 minutes, then add the white wine and allow it to boil for 2 minutes. Add parsley, saffron, and the mussels. Toss, cover, and cook on high heat for 6 minutes.

Remove from the heat. Discard any mussels that do not open. Divide the mussels between 2 soup bowls and keep warm.

Using a fine sieve, strain the broth over a saucepot. Add the cream. Bring just to a simmer. Add salt and pepper to taste.

Pour over the mussels. Served with aioli.

Serves 2.

This recipe was given to us by a good friend, Valérie Morvan. She, her husband, and two young daughters live near Paris, but she grew up in Marseilles where her grandmother made this soup "nearly always." It is a simple and delicious vegetable soup.

Soupe de Légumes "Mamie Simone"

    2 leeks, whites only, washed well and sliced thin
    2 carrots, peeled and sliced thin
    1 onion, chopped
    2 cloves garlic, minced
    1 stalk celery with leaves, sliced thin
    4 potatoes, peeled and cubed
    1 quart water or more
    2 cubes beef bouillon
      salt and pepper to taste

Place all the ingredients in a soup pot. Bring to a boil, reduce to a simmer, mix, cover, and cook for 40 minutes. If the soup is too thick, add more water.

Serves 6.

Is it is with great trepidation that I choose only one version of *Soupe au Pistou* to use here. Every homemaker has a memorized recipe that is "the best." *Soupe au Pistou* is a bean and vegetable soup very similar to Italy's minestrone. It is removed from the ordinary and elevated to the sublime by the addition of *pistou* at the last moment. *Pistou,* first cousin to Genoa's pesto but without the nuts, adds a basil and garlic fragrance that is addictive.

Our French friend, Valérie Morvan, tells us that her family eats this as a summer soup. If certain vegetables are unavailable, it's okay to omit or substitute, but *Soupe au Pistou* almost always contains the following:

Soupe au Pistou

$1/2$ cup white beans (navy, great northern, or cannellini),
    soaked overnight
3 tablespoons olive oil
2 onions, diced
3 carrots, peeled and cut into thin slices
2 stalks celery with leaves, cut into $1/2$-inch sections
2 quarts chicken stock
2 medium zucchini, sliced in $1/4$-inch pieces
2 cups Swiss chard, chopped
2 cups green beans, cut in 1-inch sections
1 tomato, peeled and diced
2 potatoes, peeled and cut into a $1/2$-inch dice
1 cup dry pasta, such as shells or elbows
    freshly ground black pepper to taste
1 recipe *pistou,* page 246
    salt

Bring the soaked beans, in their water, to a boil. Removed from the stove and let stand 1 hour. Drain and reserve the beans.

In a large soup pot, heat the oil and slowly sauté the onions for 5 minutes. Add the carrots and celery and continue to sauté for 5 more minutes.

Pour in the stock. Bring to a boil as you put the reserved white beans, zucchini, chard, green beans, tomato, and potatoes into the pot. Lower to a simmer, cover, and cook for 1 hour or until the white beans are just tender. Add the pasta and black pepper. Cook for 15 minutes more. The soup should be thick, but if it seems too thick, add a little water or stock.

In the meantime, make the *pistou*. Swirl half of the *pistou* into the soup at the last moment. Add salt to taste. Put the other half in a small bowl to pass around, so that each person can add an additional teaspoon to his soup. Serve hot.

Serves 6 to 8.

Panades are a great way to use leftover soup. They are thick with bread and are almost a casserole—a perfect lunch for the next day. They are best made with chunky soups, otherwise the overall presentation is too mushy. Construct this *panade* with leftover *Soupe au Pistou.*

Soupe au Pistou Panade

    1/2 loaf French bread, thick sliced
      1 quart leftover Soupe au Pistou
    3/4 cup grated Swiss-style cheese, such as Gruyère
    1/4 cup grated Parmesan cheese
        pistou, page 246 (optional)

Toast the bread slices on both sides under a broiler. Put half of them, single layer, in a small ovenproof casserole.

Ladle 1/2 of the soup over the bread, then 1/2 of the cheese.

Repeat with the remaining other ingredients: first, the second 1/2 of the bread, then the remaining soup, and top with remaining cheese.

Place in a preheated 350° oven for 30 minutes, or until all is hot and bubbling, and the cheese is slightly browned.

Serve with additional *pistou* if desired.

Divide and ladle into shallow soup bowls.

Serves 4.

Squash, in most of their varieties, are New World vegetables that have found their way into the cuisines of Old World France. Soups like this are called *panades,* meaning they are layered over bread and baked, often with cheese. Another *panade* is found on page 60, but this soup only uses one main vegetable—squash.

Baked Squash Panade

> 3 tablespoons olive oil
> 3 large onions, sliced
>   salt and pepper to taste
> 1/4 cup *total* fresh herbs, such as rosemary, thyme, and/or marjoram
> 1 winter squash, such as butternut or acorn, peeled, seeded, and cut in thin slices
> 1 1/2 quarts chicken stock
> 1/2 loaf country French bread, sliced
> 1/2 cup grated Parmesan cheese
> 1 cup grated Swiss-style cheese, such as Gruyère

Heat the oil and very slowly cook the onions in it for 20 minutes. Do not let them burn. Add salt, pepper, and herbs.

In the meantime, place the prepared squash in another pot with the stock. Cover and simmer for 8 minutes. Drain the squash. Reserve the stock.

Toast the bread on both sides under a broiler. In an ovenproof casserole, place 1/2 of the bread in 1 layer. Spoon 1/2 of the onions, 1/2 of the squash, and 1/2 of the cheese over the bread. Repeat with the remaining ingredients: bread, onions, squash, and cheese. Ladle 2 cups of the chicken stock evenly over all. Allow it to stand for 1 hour.

Preheat the oven to 350° and place the casserole on a middle rack to bake for 1 hour, or until hot and bubbly.

Spoon a "piece" of the soup into each bowl. Heat the remaining stock to pour over each portion.

Serves 4.

One of the most beautiful avenues in southern France is the main boulevard in Aix-en-Provence. It is tree-lined and cool, and culminates at an enormous fountain. Many years ago we were in Aix with our children, and had spent a quiet summer afternoon in a small museum and at a craft fair.

As evening came on we chose a charming outdoor restaurant on the boulevard for our dinner. We all began with a bowl of the following soup. The flavor of anise is greatly esteemed in southern France, finding its way as a vegetable, seeds, or liqueur into a wide assortment of foods—especially soups.

Cream of Fennel Soup

        4 whole fresh fennel
        2 tablespoons olive oil
        1 large onion, chopped
        1 quart chicken stock
        1 teaspoon lemon juice
        2 tablespoons anise-flavored liqueur (pernod or ouzo)
    2/3 cup heavy cream
        salt and white pepper to taste

Cut off the fennel bulbs and slice them thin. Reserve some fennel fronds for garnish. Tie the fennel stems in a bundle for the broth.

In a soup pot, heat the oil, and sauté the onion and fennel bulbs gently for 10 minutes. Do not let them burn.

Pour in the stock and the bundle of fennel stems. Bring to a boil, reduce to a simmer, cover, and cook for 40 minutes. Pick out the bundle of stems and discard.

Allow to cool somewhat, then purée the soup in batches in a blender. Strain into a clean pot. Add the lemon, liqueur, and cream. Test for salt and pepper. Reheat gently. Serve hot.

Serves 4 to 6.

It is not as usual to add cream to vegetable soups in the south of France as it is in the north, but we had a delicious cream of artichoke soup such as this one in a small restaurant in St. Paul de Vence. Artichokes, enormously popular there, are found—purple-tinged and tightly closed—in every vegetable market.

Cream of Artichoke Soup

    8 large artichoke hearts, fresh, canned, or frozen
    3 cups chicken stock
    1/4 cup fresh parsley, minced
    3/4 cup heavy cream
       salt and white pepper to taste

If you are using fresh artichokes, drop them into a large pot of salted water. Boil for about 30 minutes. Drain. When they are cool, remove all the leaves and scoop out the choke. Save only the hearts.

If you are using canned or frozen, skip the above. Put the 8 artichoke hearts to simmer, covered, in the chicken stock, for 30 minutes.

Purée the artichokes with the cooled stock in batches.

Add the parsley and cream. Add salt and pepper.

Serve hot or cold.

Serves 2 to 4.

Menton is a resort town, which lies as far east as one can go along the coast in France before entering Italy. The area, including Nice to the west, was originally part of Italy. Today it is crowded with tourists and somewhat frantic, but at the turn of the century the apartments along the main beach boulevard were fresh and lovely. We were due to return to Nice that night, but decided to stay long enough to eat. After a day on Menton's beach, we enjoyed a delicious meal of pasta and clam sauce, which began with this soup.

Spinach Soup

> 2 tablespoons olive oil
> 3 cloves garlic, sliced
> 1 large package fresh spinach, washed and chopped
> 1 quart chicken stock
> 2 potatoes, peeled and cut into 1/2-inch cubes
>   salt and pepper to taste
> 4 eggs
> 1/2 cup freshly grated Parmesan cheese

In a large pot, heat the oil and sauté the garlic for 1 minute. Put in all the spinach. Toss over high heat to wilt. Then cover, lower the heat, and let it steam for 2 minutes.

Add the stock, potatoes, salt, and pepper. Cover again and allow to simmer for 15 minutes, or until the potatoes are done.

In the meantime, gently poach 4 eggs in 1 inch of simmering, salted water in a covered fry pan. Poach for 5 minutes.

Lift out the eggs and place one into each of 4 wide shallow soup bowls. Ladle the hot soup over top. Sprinkle with grated cheese.

Serves 4.

Wild and cultivated herbs thrive in the hot dry summer climate of southern France. Long purple rows of lavender stretch into the distance, waiting to be harvested for scent and cooking. Every housewife has oregano, marjoram, sage, and thyme growing in a small garden, and parsley, basil, and chives are also nearby, ready to be snipped into a bubbling pot of soup.

Sage has always had a medicinal reputation, and this simple infusion is thought to have health-giving properties.

Sage Soup

    1 tablespoon olive oil
    5 cloves garlic, chopped
    1 quart chicken stock
    8 sage leaves
    1 teaspoon fresh thyme leaves
    1 bay leaf
    1/2 cup tiny pasta (stars or orzo)
    4 thick slices French bread

In a soup pot, heat the oil, and sauté the garlic for 1 minute. Do not let it color. Pour in the stock. Add the sage, thyme, and bay leaf. Simmer for 15 minutes.

Strain out the herbs and garlic. Return the infusion to the pot and add the pasta. Simmer for 10 minutes.

Toast the bread on both sides under a broiler. Place 1 piece in each of 4 bowls. Ladle the thin soup over top.

Serves 4.

This is a more elaborate variation of the Sage Soup on page 65. Provençale grandmothers make it to give to sick people, the old, and infants. All of its ingredients are considered to be restorative and healing. You don't have to fall into one of grandmother's categories to enjoy it!

Garlic and Herb Soup

4 cups beef stock
1 head garlic, all cloves peeled but left whole
10 sage leaves
1/4 teaspoon saffron threads
1 1/2 cups *total* sorrel and Swiss chard
    salt and pepper to taste
4 slices country-style French bread
2 tablespoons olive oil
4 eggs
1/2 cup freshly grated Parmesan cheese

Heat the beef stock. Put in the garlic and sage. Simmer for 15 minutes. Take off the heat and allow the mix to steep for 10 minutes.

Strain off the stock. Return eight cloves of garlic to the pot and mash. Add stock. Discard the rest of the garlic and the sage.

Add the saffron, sorrel, Swiss chard, salt, and pepper. Simmer for 8 minutes.

In the meantime, brush the bread with oil and toast on both sides under the broiler.

Poach the eggs in barely simmering water for 5 minutes.

Put 1 piece of bread into the bottom of each shallow soup bowl. Carefully place a poached egg on top. Then divide and ladle the hot soup over the eggs. Top with grated cheese. Serve immediately.

Serves 4.

One last variation on the herb-garlic soup theme (see pages 65 and 66), this recipe is shared with us by Jacques and Thérèse Cornetti, friends from Véséou, a tiny hamlet north of Nice. They recommend sipping this the day after a big meal.

Bay Laurel and Garlic Soup

>   5 cups water
>   6 whole cloves garlic
>   5 bay leaves
>   1 pound angel hair pasta, broken into short lengths
>   salt and pepper to taste
>   2 tablespoons olive oil

In a soup pot, bring the water to a boil, and lower to a simmer. Add the garlic and bay leaves. Cover and simmer for 20 minutes.

Crush the garlic and pick out the bay leaves. Add the broken pasta. Return to a simmer and cook for 8 minutes or until the pasta is done.

Add salt, pepper, and oil. Serve hot.

Serves 4.

This soup is similar to those found throughout coastal Spain, Italy, and France at the height of summer. We've eaten it and others like it many times—this one in an unpretentious restaurant in fashionable St. Tropez. It is meant to be a fresh, light, and quick way to use the bounty of a July garden.

Garlic and Tomato Soup

    2 tablespoons olive oil
   10 large cloves garlic, sliced
  1/2 onion, finely chopped
3 or 4 fully-ripe summer tomatoes, peeled, seeded, and diced *or*
      1 14-ounce can diced tomatoes
    3 cups chicken stock
    2 tablespoons orzo pasta
  1/2 cup fresh mixed herbs—especially parsley, basil, and
      chives, chopped
    1 teaspoon vinegar
      salt and pepper to taste

In a soup pot, heat the oil and slowly sauté the garlic and onions for 5 minutes. Do not let them brown.

Pour in the tomatoes and stock. Bring to a boil, lower to a simmer, cover, and cook for 20 minutes.

Add the orzo, herbs, vinegar, salt, and pepper. Allow it to simmer, uncovered for 10 minutes. Add additional water or stock if it is too thick. Serve hot.

Serves 4.

One summer we spent a week in the borrowed Nice apartment of a friend. We took the obligatory treks to the beach, enjoyed old Nice, wandered the streets behind the Promenade des Anglais, gaping at the 19th-century villas of the rich, and visited some museums. This time we were ready for a change.

We rented a car for two days and drove east to the Italian border, then up into the hills to see the medieval villages there. We visited Peille, Peillon, and Eze—each set like a jewel on its peak. The area of Provence just back from the coast has these and many more small towns, such as Mougins, Fayance, Moustier, and Seillan, waiting to take the visitor back in time to a simpler life. Most have spectacular views of the valley or sea. They had their genesis around the 12th century, when mountain citadels were a necessity. Here, tight warrens of streets, with homes, shops, and churches, hug the crests of mountains with small cultivated plots ringing their edge. Often the road up is torturous. Sometimes the towns realize their charm and cater to visitors with inns, restaurants, and fine crafts for sale. Sometimes a visit just offers a picture of life in Provence as it was lived in another day.

To visit Eze, the closest village to the coast, Monte Carlo, and Nice, one is required to park below and walk a steep road to the top. All of the ancient buildings have been converted into posh hotels, restaurants, and shops that cater to well-heeled clients. Its flower-filled, whitewashed streets are beautiful, but one can still discern the medieval bones of the original village.

Some years later we visited Eze and its jewel of a church once again, this time to help our friend celebrate her marriage.

No longer on the coast, the food of Haute Provence favors hearty stews and soups devoid of seafood. It is more likely to contain sausage, game, beans, and simple garden produce, such as garlic, tomatoes, cabbage, and greens. I've chosen some typical recipes that we have enjoyed on our several visits to the area. See pages 70, 71, and 73.

Épeautre Soup

  1 cup épeautre (wild wheat cereal from Provence—or substitute barley)
  1/4 cup chickpeas, soaked overnight
  1 turnip, peeled and sliced
  2 carrots, peeled and sliced into 1-inch sections
  1 leek, well washed, and cut in sections
  1 stalk celery with leaves, cut into 1-inch sections
  2 ounces thick-cut bacon, diced
  1 pound garlicky sausage, such as chourico or kielbasa
  1 onion, studded with 6 cloves
  1 meaty bone from a leg of lamb (or you may use 4 pieces of rabbit or duck)
  1 sprig thyme
  2 bay leaves
  3 cloves garlic, chopped
  3 cups chicken stock
  3 cups beef stock
    salt and freshly ground black pepper to taste
  4 tablespoons olive oil

If you are able to find dry épeautre, soak it overnight. If you are using barley, skip this step. Drain the chickpeas (and épeautre).

Put all the ingredients, except the olive oil, into a large soup pot. Bring to a boil, reduce to a simmer, cover, and cook for 2 hours.

Remove from the heat. Allow to cool. Remove the lamb bone. Pull off any remaining meat and return it to the pot. Discard the bone. Do the same if you are using rabbit or duck. Cut the sausage in 4 pieces.

Reheat the soup. Taste. It should be slightly peppery. Add more pepper if needed. Divide the meats between 4 bowls and ladle the vegetables and grain over top. Drizzle each portion with 1 tablespoon olive oil.

Serves 4.

On one of our visits to the south of France we stayed with friends who graciously spent several days showing us the sights. They live in Marseilles and are justly proud of the many treasures that lie near the coast in the areas around Nîmes, Arles, and the flat cattle-raising region of the Camargue. We clamored over the great Roman coliseum at Arles, saw a Camargue-style wedding with the men on their white horses and the women in Arlesienne costume, visited an ancient Roman quarry and monuments in the countryside, and ate a delightful picnic at the edge of a picture-perfect lavender field.

Along with history and physical beauty, food is, as always, one of Provence's attractions. This soup, a variety of *potée,* is hearty, simple, and delicious — best enjoyed as a winter dish.

Pork and Cabbage Soup (Potée)

          1/2 pound thick-sliced bacon, cubed
            2 pounds boneless pork shoulder, trimmed of fat and cut
                in 1-inch cubes
            1 large onion, chopped
            4 whole cloves garlic, peeled
            1 cup white wine
            3 cups chicken stock
            3 cups beef stock
            2 bay leaves
            2 sprigs fresh thyme
                salt and coarsely ground black pepper to taste
            1 pound garlicky sausage, such as chourico or kielbasa
            1 head Savoy cabbage, cut into 8 pieces
            6 potatoes, peeled and quartered

In a large soup pot, slowly brown the bacon. Remove and reserve the bacon. Brown the pork pieces in the remaining fat.

Add the onion and garlic. Sauté for several minutes, then add the wine. Allow it to boil and reduce for 3 minutes. Pour in the stocks, bay leaves, thyme, salt, and pepper. Return the bacon. Bring to a boil, reduce to a simmer, cover, and cook for 45 minutes.

Add the sausage and cabbage and cook for 30 minutes. Add the potatoes and cook for another 30 minutes.

Removed from the heat. Allow to cool. Cut the sausage into pieces and return to the pot. Reheat. Divide and ladle the soup into 6 bowls. Serve with lots of country bread and a green salad.

Serves 6.

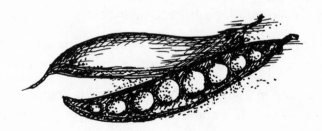

As hot and dry as the coastal summer days are along the Mediterranean, the autumn nights can become surprisingly chilly in the mountainous areas to the north. Warming stews of sausage and beans are served in the fieldstone farmhouses that dot the area. The assortment of beans used can be quite flexible.

Sausage and Bean Soup

2 cups assorted dried beans such as navy, chickpeas, kidney, and cannellini, soaked overnight
2 onions, chopped
2 cloves garlic, chopped
2 tablespoons olive oil
2 pounds assorted garlic sausage, such as bourdin, chourico, andouille, or kielbasa
2 quarts beef *or* chicken stock
2 bay leaves
2 sprigs fresh thyme
4 fresh sage leaves
2 teaspoons fresh oregano *or* marjoram
salt and pepper to taste
cooked potatoes and greens (optional)

Drain the beans after soaking overnight (do not soak split peas or lentils).

In a deep soup pot, sauté the onions and garlic in the oil. Add the sausage, beans, stock, and all the herbs and spices. Bring to a boil, reduce to a simmer, and cook, uncovered, for 1 1/2 hours, or until all the beans are tender. Add more water or stock if necessary, but this soup should be thick. Season with salt and pepper.

Cut the sausage into serving pieces and serve separately with the cooked potatoes and greens, if desired. Ladle the bean soup into bowls as a first course.

Serves 6.

Cinqueterre, Italy

The Soups of Southern Italy

. . . .

Italians are not shy about being great cooks. They are fortunate indeed, to inhabit a land that demands that they respond with wonderful foods created from its gifts. Seafood, grains, olive oil, herbs and vegetables, cheeses, and meats combine to create, along with other foods, fabulous soups. There is a spontaneity and joy in Italian soups, nurtured, I'm sure, by the ebullient personalities of their creators.

The culture of southern Italy is my personal little piece of the Mediterranean. Many of my earliest memories involved a loving grandmother, always in her kitchen, preparing the things I loved best.

We lived near my grandparents. Their house, shaded by awnings in the hot Long Island summers, almost always smelled of good things to eat. I cannot remember a visit that did not include a taste of something my grandmother said she made "just for me." My special treats included long green peppers fried in olive oil, fresh biscotti, a piece of yesterday's pizza, or perhaps one meatball, fished out of the still bubbling sauce and cut up on a plate to set before her little princess!

Some of my grandmother's best recipes were soups. I have included three of hers, along with recipes from other Italian-American friends, and recipes we have tasted in Italy.

Soups are served in Italy as part of the *primo piatti* or "first plate" course. This follows antipasti and comes before a "second plate," usually a simply prepared meat accompanied by a vegetable. *Primo piatti* are typically soups or pastas, and are considered "wet" foods.

. . . .

They always contain plentiful carbohydrates. In my grandmother's kitchen, she would cook a piece of meat in the soup or pasta sauce, then pick it out to serve separately after the soup or pasta, along with a cooked vegetable or green salad.

These "wet" first courses are a very ancient tradition—no doubt developed as a way to use stale bread. Many traditional soups are made with bread as a main ingredient. To poor peasants, bread has always been considered sacred and not to be wasted. If my grandmother dropped a piece, it was kissed when she retrieved it.

From these humble beginnings, soups have proliferated in their thousands of varieties. This book concentrates on Mediterranean soups, so we have omitted the soups of the northern and alpine regions of Italy, with their traditions of cream, butter, polenta, and rice. Our soups, from the more rural and mountainous south, are redolent of olive oil, garlic, oregano, pasta, tomatoes, hearty greens, and pork. They are in the tradition of peasant cuisines everywhere, cleverly and frugally using what is available.

In my grandparents' house, soups intended to be sopped by bread, were called *zuppa*. *Minestra* were the category of soups made with one or two, mostly green vegetables, and small or broken pasta. The grand title *minestrone* referred to those big soups which contained many kinds of vegetables, beans, and pasta. These thickened as they sat, and were often served the next day, barely warmed through.

Most Italian soups are finished by grating cheese directly into the individual bowls. With few exceptions, notably those soups that contain seafood, soups arrive with a piece of grating cheese, so that each diner can add his own at the table. The most common grating cheese in the south of Italy is some variety of pecorino (sheep's milk) cheese. "Locatelli" brand pecorino-Romano is a quality product easily found in the United States.

Over the years we have eaten seafood stews such as this in many places along Italy's west coast—Portovenere, Amalfi, and Sorrento. One we especially remember we ate in Salerno, in a little restaurant right on the coastal road. The fish soups of poor fishermen's families everywhere contain assortments of many kinds of fish, whatever is at hand. The odd fish accidentally caught with the others, too-small fish, or other unsaleable creatures find their way into the pot. The soups we have enjoyed are usually flavorful mixtures of tomatoes, garlic, and five or six kinds of seafood. With a salad, this stew is a complete meal.

Italian Seafood Stew

- 1/2 cup olive oil
- 1 onion, chopped
- 1 carrot, peeled and sliced thin
- 1 stalk celery, sliced thin
- 1/2 cup dry white wine
- 2 quarts chicken stock
- 1/4 teaspoon hot red pepper flakes
- 2 ripe tomatoes, peeled, seeded, and chopped, *or* 1 14-ounce can diced tomatoes
- 12 mussels, well scrubbed
- 12 clams, well scrubbed
- 1 large lobster tail, in its shell
- 12 large shrimp, shelled
- 1 1/2 pounds assorted firm white fish, cut in 1-inch pieces
- 2 squid (calamari), cleaned and cut into 1/4-inch rings (see note, page 37)
  salt to taste
- 8 1-inch thick pieces crusty Italian bread
- 2 cloves garlic, peeled
- 1/2 cup fresh parsley, chopped

In a large soup pot, heat all but 2 tablespoons of the oil. Sauté the onion, carrot, and celery for 5 minutes. Pour in the wine and allow it to boil and reduce for several minutes.

Add the stock, pepper, and tomatoes. Cover and gently cook for 45 minutes.

In the meantime, steam the mussels and clams in a bit of water in a covered pot for 5 minutes. Discard any that do not open. Remove to a bowl. Strain all of the liquid in their pot into the soup pot.

After 45 minutes, put the lobster tail into the soup. Cook it for 8 minutes. Remove. When it has cooled, take it out of its shell, and slice the meat.

Add the shrimp and fish pieces to the soup. Cook gently for several minutes. Add the squid. Cook for 2 more minutes. Remove from the heat.

Add the reserved mussels, clams, and lobster. Add salt if desired. Allow the soup to sit for 10 minutes.

In the meantime, toast the bread on both sides under the broiler. Rub each piece on both sides with garlic and brush with the reserved olive oil.

Place 1 piece of bread in the bottom of each wide soup bowl. Ladle the soup over the bread, and divide the seafood so that everyone gets some of each kind. Sprinkle with fresh parsley. Serve hot.

Serves 8.

Italy juts far out into the Mediterranean and her coastal towns and cities have many wonderful seafood soups. We ate this unforgettable soup one night at a small outdoor restaurant in Rome.

On that hot August evening when only the tourists were still in town, we walked several miles from our hotel, crossed the Tiber on an old Roman bridge, and wandered deep into the worker's district of Trastevere to the Piazza Santa Maria. The golden mosaic facade of the 12th-century church fairly glowed, while neighbors hung out of windows to watch as young boys practiced their soccer moves around the historic fountain.

Mussel Soup

> 4 tablespoons olive oil
> 3 or 4 cloves garlic, minced
> 3/4 cup dry white wine
> 1/2 cup fresh parsley, chopped
> 2 cups chicken stock
> salt and freshly ground black pepper to taste
> 4 dozen mussels, cleaned
> 4 thick pieces crusty rustic-style Italian bread, toasted
> additional chopped parsley, for a garnish

In a large covered pot, heat the oil and sauté the garlic for 2 minutes. Do not let it brown.

Pour in the wine and boil until its reduces by half. Add the parsley, chicken stock, salt, and pepper.

With the liquid at a full boil, add the mussels. Toss them for 1 minute in the liquid. Then cover tightly, lower the heat by half, and allow them to cook for 6 minutes.

Open the pot, toss again, and discard any mussels that do not open.

Set out 4 wide soup bowls, place a piece of toasted bread in each, and evenly divide the mussels in their opened shells over top.

Using a strainer lined with 2 layers of cheesecloth, strain all the liquid out of the pot into a deep bowl. The mussels will have released some liquid of their own. Discard any sand caught in the cloth and divide the "soup" into the four bowls of the mussels and bread. Sprinkle with the remaining parsley. Serve at once.

Serves 4.

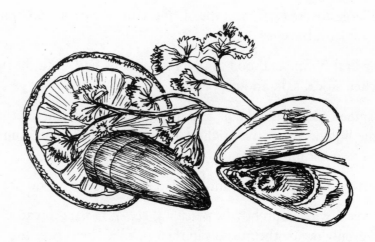

When my mother was a child, she and my grandmother would go out together to gather the first dandelion shoots of the spring. After sharing some with a dear family friend they called "aunt," the rest would be brought home and used in a rich chicken soup that was always served for Easter dinner. This is my grandmother's recipe as my mother Marie remembers it. Make this soup one day ahead.

Grandma's Easter Sunday Soup

The soup:

    1 3-pound chicken, ready for the pot
    1 onion, chopped
2 or 3 carrots, peeled and cut into rounds
2 or 3 stalks celery with leaves, cut into 1/2-inch pieces
    2 bay leaves
  1/3 cup fresh parsley, chopped
      salt and pepper to taste
    1 pound washed and trimmed dandelion greens

Place all ingredients, except the greens, in a big soup pot. Cover with water. Bring to a boil, lower to a simmer, and cook for 1 hour.

Remove the chicken and allow it to cool. Cut off about 1/2 pound of meat and shred or chop coarsely. Return it to the pot. Save the rest of the chicken for another meal.

Refrigerate the soup for 24 hours, then pick as much of the congealed chicken fat off the top of the cold soup as you wish. Add the greens and bring the soup to a boil. Lower to a simmer.

In the meantime make the meatballs as follows:

  3/4 pound lean ground beef
    1 egg
2 to 3 tablespoons grated pecorino cheese
    3 tablespoons fresh bread crumbs
  1/3 cup fresh parsley, finely chopped

1 clove garlic, minced
salt and pepper to taste

In a bowl, mix and knead all the ingredients together until smooth. Break off small pieces, and roll them into balls about the size of a hazelnut. Slip them into the gently simmering soup, and allow them to poach for 7 to 10 minutes.

Remove the soup from the stove and allow it to rest awhile. Serve hot. Pass a bowl of freshly grated pecorino cheese to be sprinkled on top.

Serves 6 as a first course.

Note: Do not gather dandelions past mid-spring; do not gather from pesticide-sprayed areas.

Along with the omnipresence fig tree, carefully wrapped against the cold in winter, my grandparents also kept a small chicken coop for fresh eggs and the occasional old hen for the pot. When my grandmother picked up her basket to gather a few eggs, I always begged to tag along, even though their flapping and squawking never failed to frighten me.

Fresh eggs and chicken broth are the main ingredients in *stracciatella* or "rag soup," a classic throughout Italy. Wonderfully simple, this delicate soup has been modified in many ways by many cooks over the years. Often cheese, fresh herbs, and breadcrumbs are added.

Stracciatella

4 cups chicken stock
3 large eggs
1¹/3 cup fresh bread crumbs (not packaged ones)
¹/3 cup freshly grated pecorino cheese
salt and freshly ground pepper to taste
¹/4 cup parsley, minced

Bring the stock to a boil. Beat together the eggs, bread crumbs, cheese, salt, and pepper.

Remove the stock from the heat and pour in the egg mixture. Blend well with a whisk. Return the stock to the heat, bring to a boil, and continue to whisk for 2 minutes.

Serve immediately. Sprinkle each bowl with some parsley.

Serves 4.

In Apulia, in the deep south of Italy, there are two towns, seldom visited, that each have a distinctive way of constructing their homes.

One, Matera, sits on a mountain in a poor, rocky, and quite desolate area of deep ravines. Lacking forests for wood, hundreds of years ago the people began to live in homes built directly into the rock caves and depressions of their mountain. Today, in the old part of town, now largely deserted, sit hundreds of dwellings consisting of manmade fronts that become almost indistinguishable from the mountain as they merge with their cave backs. We spent several hours wandering up the roads that circle the mountain and exploring the small deserted homes.

Later that day we drove fifty miles to Alberobello, a town in the heel of the peninsula. It contains nearly one thousand *trulli*—strange, round, white dry-stone structures with conical roofs. They are sometimes grouped or connected, and their outsides are decorated with crosses and other symbols. There are smaller unpainted versions in the fields near town. Some of the trulli within the town have been converted into shops and restaurants.

The specialty pasta shape of the district around Alberobello is called *orecchiette* or "little ears." We ate this soup of "little ears" in a *trulli* restaurant there.

Chicken Soup with Orecchiette

> 1/4 pound pancetta or bacon, diced
> 1 large onion, chopped
> 1 large carrot, peeled and cut into thin rounds
> 1 large stalk celery with leaves, cut in 1/2-inch pieces
> 1/2 chicken, about 1 1/2 pounds
> 1 bay leaf
> 1 1/2 quarts water
> salt and pepper to taste
> 2 tomatoes, peeled, seeded, and diced, *or* 1 14-ounce can diced tomatoes

1 medium zucchini, sliced into 1/4-inch rounds
1/3 pound orecchiette pasta
1/2 cup freshly grated pecorino cheese

In a large soup pot, brown the pancetta. Then sauté the onion, carrot, and celery in the fat in the pot (add a bit of olive oil if it is too dry).

Put the chicken and bay leaf in the pot and pour in the water. Add salt and pepper to taste. Add the tomatoes, bring to a boil, reduce to a simmer, cover, and cook for 1 hour.

Remove the chicken. Allow it to cool a bit and remove some of the meat. Shred or chop it and return it to the soup. Reserve the rest of the chicken for another use.

Add the zucchini. Simmer for 10 minutes. Add the pasta at this time and cook all for 10 minutes more, or until the pasta is done.

Ladle into bowls and sprinkle each with some grated cheese.

Serves 6.

In the United States, every small Italian restaurant seems able to serve up a steaming bowl of minestrone. It is the most instantly recognizable and popular Italian soup. Minestrone is a vegetable soup, thick and hardy, with as many variations as there are restaurants and cooks. In the south, most contain white beans, fresh herbs such as basil and marjoram, and sometimes hot red pepper flakes.

My grandmother's minestrone came right from her garden. A container of it was usually shared with our household the next day, when it tasted even better.

The frugal trick of cooking a cheese rind in the soup is common in Italian households. It enhances the flavor but is taken out before serving.

Minestrone

    1/8 pound pancetta or bacon, diced
    2 tablespoons olive oil
    1 clove garlic, minced
    1 onion, chopped
    1 stalk celery, cut into 1/2-inch pieces
    1 carrot, peeled and cut into 1/4-inch rounds
    1 1/2 quarts water *or* chicken stock
    1 small zucchini, cut into 1/4-inch rounds
    1 large tomato, peeled, seeded, and diced
    1/3 head of cabbage, sliced into 1/4-inch shreds
    1/2 teaspoon dry marjoram *or* oregano
    1/4 teaspoon hot red pepper flakes
    2-inch x 4-inch piece of pecorino cheese rind (optional)
    salt to taste
    1 potato, peeled and cut into 1/2-inch cubes
    1 14-ounce can cannellini or navy beans, drained
    1/2 cup pasta, such as short tubes or small shells
    1/2 cup fresh basil, chopped
    1/2 cup freshly grated pecorino cheese

In a large soup pot, sauté the pancetta for 3 minutes. Add the oil, garlic, onion, celery, and carrot. Continue to sauté for 3 more minutes over high heat.

Pour in the water or stock, zucchini, tomato, cabbage, herbs, pepper, and cheese rind. Bring to a boil, cover, and cook at a simmer for 30 minutes.

Uncover, salt to taste, and add the potato and beans. Cook for 10 minutes. Add the pasta and basil and cook for another 10 minutes. Test again for sufficient salt.

This soup is wonderful served the next day. If served the same day, allow it to rest for an hour. Pick out the cheese rind and reheat the soup gently. Serve with grated cheese on top and lots of fresh bread.

Serves 6.

Many vegetables commonly enjoyed in Italy, and by Italian-Americans, have not even been known by other Americans until recently. Broccoli rabe or rapini, artichokes, cardoons, and fennel come to mind.

Fennel looks somewhat like a fat bulb of celery, but it has a pronounced anise flavor. As a child, I most clearly remember it served raw as part of a relish plate each Thanksgiving. However, I like it better cooked, when the flavor becomes more subtle. It is delicious braised with butter. Its seeds flavor sausage dishes and its delicate fronds are used as a decorative garnish. Fennel soups like this one are common in Italy.

Fennel Soup

2 ounces pancetta or bacon, cut into a small dice
1 tablespoon olive oil
1 bulb fennel, trimmed of its stalks and fronds, sliced thin
1 large onion, chopped
1 clove garlic, minced
1 quart chicken stock
1 medium potato, peeled and cut into a 1/2-inch dice
1 14-ounce can navy or cannellini beans, drained
salt and pepper to taste
1/2 cup freshly grated pecorino cheese

In a large soup pot, sauté the pancetta for 3 minutes. Add the oil, fennel, onion, and garlic. Continue to sauté for 3 more minutes, then pour in the stock. Bring to a boil, reduce to a simmer, cover, and cook for 20 minutes.

Add the potato. Cook for 10 minutes.

Add the beans and cook for 5 minutes. Add salt and pepper to taste. Remove from the heat and let the soup rest for 20 minutes.

Serve with cheese sprinkled on top—and with lots of crusty Italian bread.

Serves 4.

My favorite "Italian" vegetable is broccoli rabe or *rapini*. In the cabbage family, it is a dark-green cross between broccoli and turnip greens. The flavor is strong, slightly bitter and, to me, very addictive. I love it best the way I used to beg my grandmother to cook it— quickly sautéed in olive oil with garlic and salt, then covered and steamed in its own juice for twenty minutes. The next day, between two slices of Italian bread, it made a sandwich from heaven.

It is often combined with cooked, thinly sliced, fresh pork sausage as a sauce for pasta. This simple version uses sausage and turns it into a soup.

Rapini and Sausage Soup

```
1 1/2  pounds fresh rapini
  1/3  cup olive oil
    3  large cloves garlic, sliced thin
    1  quart chicken stock
    1  pound Italian-style fresh pork sausage
       salt and pepper to taste
    4  1-inch thick pieces day-old Italian bread
  1/2  cup grated pecorino cheese
```

Wash the rapini in several changes of water. If the stems are very long, remove 1 or 2 inches. Chop the rapini into large sections.

Heat the oil in a soup pot. Add the garlic and gently sauté for 2 minutes. Add the rapini and stock.

In the meantime, remove the casing from the sausage. Break it up and fry in a separate pan, until it is no longer pink and begins to brown. Add it to the soup. Bring the soup to a boil, reduce the heat, cover, and allow it to simmer for 30 minutes. Add salt and pepper to taste.

Toast the bread on both sides under the broiler. Place 1 piece in each serving bowl and ladle the hot soup over the top. Sprinkle each serving with grated cheese.

Serves 4.

One afternoon we boarded a plane in New York. After flying all
night, we arrived in Rome in the early morning—Roman time. With
only a few hours sleep, we decided to rent a car and leave the hot
city. We traveled east into the Abruzzi, and finally stopped late in the
afternoon in Scanno, a mountain town of some reputation for its
charm.

The weather was cool at this higher elevation. We parked and
walked the steep, narrow, nearly deserted streets. Women sat on their
doorsteps chatting and making lace. Their nimble fingers moved
dozens of bobbins and pins over firm black pillows on their laps. The
beautiful white lace, in all its intricacy, formed as they worked. They
seemed to scarcely look; it was as though their fingers had memorized the patterns. We watched with fascination. More astonishing
to us was what they were wearing. They were clothed in somber, long

Scanno, Italy

black dresses, and each had a black scarf tied to form a huge bow behind her head. We felt that we had stepped into another age. Had we not just left New York?

It had been 24 hours of airline food and we were starving. At the top of the town there was an inn overlooking a valley. We entered. At first not a soul was in sight. Finally a woman washing the stone floor told us she could find us some food. Not knowing what to expect, we sat at a table on the terrace. She brought some crusty bread and two steaming bowls of a cabbage and sausage soup. We were exhausted and this meal was what we needed. It was delicious.

Sausage and Cabbage Soup

1 pound fresh Italian-style pork sausage pieces, left in their casings
1 large onion, chopped
2 tablespoons olive oil
2 cloves garlic, chopped
1½ quarts chicken stock
1 small head Savoy cabbage, cut into 1-inch pieces
2 medium potatoes, peeled and cut into ½-inch cubes

In a large soup pot, slowly brown the sausage and onion in the oil. Add the garlic and continue to cook for several more minutes.

Pour in the stock and add the cabbage. Bring to a boil, reduce to a simmer, cover, and cook at a low simmer for 40 minutes. Add the potatoes and cook for 15 minutes more.

Like most soups, this improves as it sits. Make it in the afternoon, or even the day before, for an evening meal. Reheat. Serve with lots of crusty bread.

Serves 6.

This version of a classic southern Italian soup was given to me by Annamarie Rollo, whose family is originally from the Naples area. She told me that this is her grandmother's recipe and that her family has made this soup for generations.

Escarole and White Bean Soup (Minestra e Fagioli)

        2 or 3 heads of escarole
            3 tablespoons olive oil
    3 or 4 large cloves garlic, chopped
                hot red pepper flakes to taste
        1½ pounds Italian sausage
            2 large cans chicken stock, *or* 3 quarts homemade
            2 14-ounce cans white beans (navy, cannellini, or white
                kidney beans)
                salt to taste

Clean and wash the escarole several times in a large basin of water. Drain and roughly chop.

In a large pot, heat the olive oil and sauté the garlic for 2 minutes. Add the hot pepper flakes and the escarole. Cover and cook for 15 minutes over low heat, until wilted. Set aside.

In a sauté pan, cook the sausage in 1 cup of water, until the water evaporates and the sausage browns on both sides. Allow it to cool a bit, then slice into ½-inch rounds.

Pour the chicken stock into a large soup pot. Add all the wilted escarole, olive oil, garlic, and juices. Add the sausage pieces and their juices.

Drain and rinse the canned beans. Add to the soup pot. Cook everything together for 30 minutes. Serve with crusty Italian bread and freshly grated pecorino cheese on top.

Serves 8.

Years ago we were in Calabria, in Italy's "toe," visiting relatives in Cervicati, the hometown of my grandfather. We located it with difficulty—a tiny town, unchanged since my grandfather left at 15 years old.

Miles passed as we climbed hot, dusty, unpaved roads, up and up into the rugged mountains. Finally we were there. In the town square, chickens scratched around the public spigot and several old man sat talking outside a small shop. We had names and photos, a letter of introduction, and were to deliver some gifts from relatives.

Once it was clear who we were, we spent the rest of the day being hosted in house after house, eating delicious food, comparing photos, and talking as well as we all could to each other. What a wonderful day it was!

One of the stories that day concerned conditions in these mountains during the poorest days of World War II. They told us that there was nothing to eat; that they might work all day in exchange for a bushel of onions, then have nothing but onion soup for a week! The following soup is a close duplicate of just such a peasant's soup.

Calabrian Onion Soup

> 4 ounces pancetta or bacon, cut into a small dice
> 2 tablespoon olive oil
> 3 or 4 large onions, sliced thin
> 3 or 4 garlic cloves, chopped
> several sprigs fresh herbs such as marjoram, thyme, or oregano
> 1 1/2 quarts chicken stock
> salt to taste
> hot red pepper flakes to taste
> thick slices crusty rustic-style Italian bread
> freshly grated pecorino cheese

In a large soup pot, fry the pancetta or bacon until crisp. Drain off some of the fat. Set the pancetta aside.

In the same pot, heat the olive oil and sauté the onions and garlic for several minutes. Add the herbs, the reserved pancetta, the stock, salt, and pepper flakes. Cook, uncovered, on a low simmer for 1 hour. Add more stock if needed.

Place 1 thick piece of bread in each soup bowl. Ladle the hot soup over the bread, and sprinkle liberally with cheese. Serve immediately.

Serves 4.

Note: I doubt that my relatives would have had pancetta in 1943, and I'm sure they had to substitute water for the chicken stock!

One day I asked my grandfather how his mother made bread before the days of neatly packaged yeast. He told me that all the women of his village agreed on who would bake bread on a particular day of the week. Then it was a simple matter of transferring, street to street, a small, unbaked portion of starter dough each day to the designated women.

Bread, garlic, and olive oil make up a trio of ancient and indispensable ingredients in southern Italian cooking. My friend, Mike Rollo, related to me how his family, living near Naples, obtained their olive oil. Olives are picked from the trees, and gathered from the ground in late autumn. Their trees are scattered over many small plots. Nets are spread to catch the olives, but each must be picked up by hand, often by pushing through ice and snow.

After gathering, they are stored in a warm place for several days before they are pressed. This wait yields the very best oil from the first pressing.

Extra virgin olive oil such as this, fat heads of garlic, and thick slices of day-old bread combine to make this quintessentially Mediterranean soup. It is frugal, earthy, and delicious.

Garlic and Bread Soup

      4 tablespoons olive oil
      1 entire head garlic, each clove peeled
  1 1/2 quarts chicken stock
  1/4 teaspoon hot red pepper flakes
         salt to taste
  1/4 cup fresh parsley, chopped
      6 1-inch thick pieces day-old Italian bread
  1/2 cup freshly grated pecorino cheese

Heat 2 tablespoons of the oil in a large soup pot. Reserve 2 cloves of garlic. Chop the rest and lightly sauté for 1 minute in the oil.

Add the stock, pepper, and salt. Bring to a boil, reduce to a simmer, cover, and cook for 1 hour. Remove from the heat, mash the garlic, and immediately add the parsley.

In the meantime, toast the bread on both sides under the broiler. Rub each side of the toasted bread with the reserved garlic cloves. Then brush each side with the reserved olive oil.

Place a piece in each of 6 soup bowls and ladle the soup over them. Sprinkle each bowl with some of the cheese. Serve hot.

Serves 6.

Today's restaurants spare no effort or expense to include the most chic Mediterranean ingredients in their menus, as though their chefs had just discovered them.

I often reflect on the wealth of these ingredients my grandparents routinely used. Their garden was always planted with lots of basil, enough for every meal in summer, with plenty to spare for drying. Fresh arugula and dandelion greens were gathered from local fields by my mother and grandmother. There was an abundance of fresh garden tomatoes, a portion of which were cut open to sun-dry on trays. Pine nuts found their way into meatballs, stuffed artichokes, and *braciola* (rolled meat). My favorite cooked vegetable was broccoli rabe or *rapini*. Biscotti were made several times a month. My grandfather often made a kind of bread salad—big slices of crusty, toasted Italian bread, dressed with balsamic vinegar, olive oil, salt, pepper, oregano, basil, and ripe tomatoes. I loved it! My grandmother sometimes made homemade pizza and pasta, and if someone in the family was traveling into "the city," he would buy the best mozzarella. My grandfather sniffed that the packaged stuff tasted like erasers!

The following is similar to my grandfather's bread salad—same taste, different form.

Bread and Tomato Soup with Basil

        10 1-inch slices from a crusty French baguette
         2 large cloves peeled garlic, cut in half
         2 14-ounce cans diced tomatoes, *or* 6 very ripe summer
             tomatoes, peeled, seeded, and diced
2 or 3 cups fat-free chicken stock
         1/2 cup packed basil leaves, chopped
         1/3 cup extra virgin olive oil
         2 tablespoons balsamic vinegar
         1/2 teaspoon dried oregano
             salt and coarsely ground pepper to taste

Toast the bread on both sides in the oven. Rub each side with a garlic clove to "grate" on the garlic flavor. Cut the small bread rounds into quarters to make 40 approximately 1-inch pieces.

Place all the ingredients in a large pot. Toss to coat and refrigerate for 30 minutes. If you want to make it more soupy, add more water or stock before serving.

You can serve this soup hot, too. Just hold back the basil, oil, vinegar, oregano, salt, and pepper until after you have heated the garlic bread and tomatoes in the stock.

Serves 4 or 6.

Southern Italians are very partial to cardoons, which resemble very big heads of celery. They are slightly fuzzy, and a pale soft green. Each stalk must be peeled, and often they are parboiled, then battered and fried. They lend themselves well to soups too, but their taste is subtle and easily overpowered by other strong ingredients.

Cardoon Soup

        1/4 pound pancetta or bacon, cut into a small dice
         2 tablespoons olive oil
         1 medium onion, chopped
         1 carrot, peeled and sliced into thin rounds
         1 large ripe tomato, peeled, seeded, and chopped
       1 1/2 quarts chicken stock
     6 or 7 stalks cardoon, peeled
         2 eggs
           salt and pepper to taste
         8 large slices crusty Italian bread
         2 cloves garlic, peeled
        1/2 cup freshly grated pecorino cheese

In a large soup pot, slowly sauté the pancetta in the oil. Add the onion and carrot. Continue to cook until they are lightly browned. Add the tomato and stock. Bring to a boil and reduce to a simmer.

In the meantime, cut the peeled cardoons into 1/2-inch slices and immediately add to the simmering soup, before they can turn brown.

Cover the soup and allow it to cook for 30 to 40 minutes. Scramble the eggs with salt and pepper. Swirl into the simmering soup. Continue to cook for 2 or 3 minutes more.

Under the broiler, toast the bread on both sides until lightly browned. Rub each side with the garlic. Place one piece in the bottom of each soup bowl. Ladle the soup over the bread. Serve immediately with freshly grated pecorino cheese on top.

Serves 6 to 8.

The category of soups called *acquacotta,* literally "cooked water," is found everywhere, with as many variations as cooks. Generally, they are vegetable soups made with water rather than stock, then thickened with eggs and cheese. Sometimes one or two vegetables predominate.

We had been touring Herculaneum, near Naples. It was the other town buried in the disastrous eruption of Vesuvius in 79 A.D.; the more well-known Pompeii was also buried that day. To tour the 2,000-year-old town where archaeologists continue to uncover new wonders, one must park in the town of Ercolano, which has grown up more or less over the site, then walk a long ramp down into the old Roman city. As in Pompeii, one is free to walk through streets, houses, shops, baths, and temples, all frozen in time.

Several hours passed quickly and we returned to Ercolano for a late lunch. My great-grandmother's last name was Ercolano; we are sure that generations earlier her people came from that town, so near to Sorrento where my grandmother was born.

Up a quiet side street in a small restaurant, we had bowls of steaming *acquacotta funghi,* or mushroom soup.

Mushroom Soup

> 1/4 pound pancetta or bacon, diced
> 2 cloves garlic, minced
> 2 tablespoons olive oil
> 3/4 pound fresh portobella *or* porcini mushrooms
> 1/4 teaspoon dried thyme *or* marjoram
> 1 quart water
> 1 medium tomato, peeled, seeded, and diced
>   salt and pepper to taste
> 3 eggs
> 1/2 cup freshly grated pecorino cheese
> 1/4 cup fresh parsley, minced

In a soup pot, sauté the pancetta for 3 minutes. Add the garlic and olive oil and continue to sauté for 3 more minutes.

Wipe any dirt off the mushrooms with a damp cloth. Cut the mushrooms into thin slices and add to the pot. Sauté for 2 minutes.

Add the herbs, water, tomato, salt, and pepper. Bring to a boil, reduce to a simmer, cover, and cook for 30 minutes.

Mix the eggs and cheese together. Remove the pot from the heat. Pour in the egg mix. Continue to stir. Return the pot to the heat and bring to a boil.

Take the pot off the heat and allow it to rest for 10 minutes. Ladle into bowls and sprinkle each with parsley.

Serves 4.

Mike Rollo, a friend who was born and grew up near Naples, shared his family's recipe for lentil soup with me. In the winter, when a fire was always burning in the hearth, his mother would fill a clay jug with these ingredients and pushed it close to the heat. There it would remain, slowly cooking all day. Hers took seven to nine hours, but with some modifications we can duplicate it in our modern kitchens.

Neapolitan Lentil Soup

    1 package (2 cups) brown lentils
    1 large clove garlic, chopped
  3/4 pound smoked pig's feet, a smoked ham bone with some
      meat, or smoked pork sausage
 2¹/2 quarts water
  1/4 cup mixed fresh herbs such as oregano, thyme, or sage,
      chopped
      hot red pepper flakes to taste
  1/2 cup dry small pasta, such as orzo or stars
      salt to taste
      olive oil

Place the lentils, garlic, smoked meat, and water in a large pot. Bring just to a low simmer, and allow it to slowly cook about 1 hour, or until the lentils are tender. Add water if necessary.

Add the fresh herbs, hot red pepper flakes, pasta, and salt. Allow to simmer for another 15 minutes. Remove from the heat and rest the soup for an hour or overnight.

Pick the meat off the bone, and return it to the soup. Discard the bone. Reheat the soup. Serve hot with a little extra virgin olive oil drizzled over the top.

Serves 6.

Note: My grandmother, from Sorrento, near Naples, made a similar soup. She omitted the hot red pepper and pasta, but did add a few generous handfuls of fresh spinach or escarole leaves in the last 15 minutes.

Small pasta (short tube or shell shapes), combines with white beans, such as navy or cannellini, to make the popular *pasta e fagioli*. It is a meal in a bowl. Often served the next day when it has thickened, sometimes it is just warmed, but it is always served topped with freshly grated pecorino cheese. This version is my grandmother's from Campania (Naples). Hers always contained tomatoes, which my grandfather brought in from the garden.

I remember watching my grandfather start the following year's tomato plants. In the late autumn he would let several of his best tomatoes grow overripe and heavy. After they fell to the ground, he would crush and smear them underfoot, exposing the seeds to the sun. When they were dry, he would gather them or just cover them with mulch, and months later they would sprout in the warm spring air.

Pasta and Bean Soup (Pasta e Fagioli)

    3 tablespoons olive oil
  1/4 pound pancetta or bacon, cut into a small dice
    1 large onion, chopped
    1 stalk celery, chopped
    3 large cloves garlic, chopped
    3 very ripe tomatoes, peeled, seeded, and chopped, *or* 1
      14-ounce can diced tomatoes
    1 quart or more chicken stock
    1 14-ounce can cannellini beans, drained
  3/4 cup dry pasta, short tubes or small shells
  1/2 cup fresh basil leaves, chopped
      salt and pepper to taste
  1/2 cup freshly grated pecorino cheese

Heat the olive oil in a large soup pot. Sauté the pancetta, onion, celery, and garlic gently for 8 minutes. Add the tomatoes and stock. Simmer for 15 minutes.

Add the beans, pasta, and basil. Cook for 10 minutes more. Add salt and pepper if needed. The soup should be thick, and will continue to thicken the next day, but add more stock if you wish.

Serve at once, or reheat the next day. Sprinkle with cheese.

Serves 6.

Santorini, Greece

The Soups of
Greece and Turkey

∙∙∙

Continuing on our clockwise journey around the Mediterranean, which began in Portugal and Spain and will conclude in North Africa, we now proceed to Greece, then Turkey. Since as early as 1000 B.C., these two areas have been closely related, beginning with the settlement of western Turkey by the ancient Greeks, who considered both sides of the Aegean their land. These were not mere colonies, but fully developed cities such as Pergamum, Ephesus, and Aphrodisias. Their close alliance continued through the Roman era and early Christianity. It was only in the centuries after the Muslims arrived that the two areas began to diverge. Today, for the vast majority of citizens, Greece is Christian and Turkey is Muslim.

The cuisines are quite similar too, although not the same. One noticeable difference is the religious absence of pork and wine in Turkey. Both cuisines, however, are clearly looking in two directions, to the west with its European traditions and to the traditions of the Middle East.

To travel from Spain, Italy, or France to Greece is to taste this difference. Here the food is more clear and defined; the pure flavor of dill or lemon, the sharp saltiness of olives served alone, the crisp crackle of phyllo pastry dripping with unctuous honey, tangy fresh yogurt over a sweet melon—each flavor stands alone and demands attention.

The colors of Greece are blue and white. The cloudless blue sky, immaculate, whitewashed buildings, the deepest navy blue of its waters, even its flag, bear witness to this. The landscape of much of Greece is dry and severe, a test of any people to grow and flourish. Yet the Greeks seem to relish the challenge and have found the few crops and animals that they can use to feed themselves. Much of their food comes from the sea. On the land they grow olives, figs, nuts, lemons, and oranges. From the fields they gather herbs that seem to thrive in the arid conditions, such as thyme, oregano, bay leaves, sage, marjoram, and rosemary. In their small gardens, with a minimum of water, they can raise parsley, garlic, dill, and chives. Free for the taking are pine nuts, honey, capers, fennel, and juniper berries. Eggplant, peppers, onions, and tomatoes, a few chickens for meat and eggs, perhaps a goat or sheep for cheese, meat, and milk—the farmers and fishermen of Greece, though poor, eat well.

Along with Italy and Spain, Greece leads the world in olive oil production, though they consume most of it themselves. The wonderful olive tree, which produces fruit and oil for hundreds of years, is planted by the millions across the landscape. The oil, with its healthful properties, finds its way into virtually every dish. The best olives come from Kalamata, in the Peloponnesus, in southern Greece.

We have often noticed the almost obsessive concern Americans have with nearly everything that they eat. Is it good for their heart or cholesterol level, is it too fattening, too salty, too much meat, too sweet, too starchy? Does it have enough vitamins, do we need supplements, does one need to lose weight, gain weight?

Throughout the Mediterranean, perhaps especially in Greece, people are also intimately involved with their food. But there is a critical difference. In Greece, lots of families raise at least some of their fresh foods on small plots, or even on rooftops in the city. From an early age, children are involved in raising a lamb or chickens, picking olives, gathering herbs, pine nuts, or capers, drying figs or raisins, or making yogurt. As for the questions that hound every American meal, they are blessedly free of them, and at peace with their foods. They see food as a joy, not as a medicine, preferring instead to bless and enjoy the gifts of their land and sea.

Soup, for the Greeks, starts a meal, or, if it is very hearty, comprises the whole meal. Some soups are traditionally served on religious holidays. Fairly limited in number, they are without the endless variety found in some cuisines.

Turkish cuisine is more complex than that of Greece. Their land is more bountiful and some of their dishes have the advantage of having been developed for the Ottoman rulers at the court of Topkapi, in Istanbul. A strong theme in Turkish cooking is the eastern influence, carried there by caravans, nomads, warriors, and settlers through the ages. Foods and spices such as rice, allspice, cumin, and black pepper arrived in this way. They also have the early influence of the Romans, who taught them how to obtain olive oil and introduced them to their more western foods.

The soups of Turkey, as with all their foods, are more varied than the ones of their neighbor to the west, a result of the east-west trade of goods, ideas, and people, that criss-crossed Anatolia over the millennia. Both cuisines, Greek and Turkish, are truly Mediterranean, with their reliance on olive oil and garlic as dominant flavors, and the exuberance, purity, and joy with which they prepare and eat their foods.

Fisherman, Greece

Greek Soups

Our trip to Greece was to include a car trip south into the Peloponnesus, but like all visitors by air or sea, we had to begin in Athens. We decided to deal with jet lag by staying put for a few days, and seeing Athens' sights at our leisure.

Having been warned about the heat and crowds of summer, we arrived on a sparkling day in October. Over the next several days we toured the Acropolis, several wonderful antiquity museums, the historic Plaka and Anafiotika districts, the Turkish market, and the Roman agora. Athens is a sprawling city of hundreds of residential neighborhoods, but virtually all of the areas of interest are within walking distance. Our hotel was in a good location off Constitution Square and we never needed a bus or cab.

The first night of our visit to Athens, we ate in a small neighborhood restaurant recommended by our hotel. We arrived early, and sat, sipping glasses of *retsina,* in a tiny arbor-covered backyard, waiting for the two proprietors to finish cooking. Although we have never grown to enjoy the taste of resin-flavored retsina wine, the rest of the meal was a pure joy. We started with the familiar Greek classic of lemon-scented *avgolemono* soup, then had a rather unusual *saganaki* or fried cheese, then each of us had a perfectly prepared baby lamb chop with fried potatoes.

Avgolemono is really a lemon and egg sauce, which is added to many soups at the last minute to thicken and enrich them. It deserves a separate recipe (page 249) and is often used by itself over vegetables, fish, and meats. It is possible to eat *avgolemono* soup that contains various combinations of vegetables, rice, chicken, and meats. The version we ate this time is the most often prepared, both in Greece and in Turkey. Its recipe, and several other variations follow.

Chicken and Rice Soup with Avgolemono

    1 quart chicken stock
    1/3 cup raw white rice
    2 eggs
       juice of 1 lemon, about 4 tablespoons
       salt and pepper to taste

In a saucepot, bring the stock to a boil. Add the rice. Reduce to a simmer and cook, covered, for 17 minutes exactly.

In a bowl, whisk the egg and lemon juice together well. Slowly add 1 cup of the hot stock, continuing to whisk.

Return the *avgolemono* to the rice soup. Mix well, as you slowly raise the heat to just below boiling. The soup will thicken enough to coat the spoon. Serve hot.

Serves 4.

Variation: Poach a small half chicken breast (about 4 ounces) in the chicken stock as you cook the rice. Remove, shred or chop the meat, and return to the soup. Continue exactly as per the above recipe.

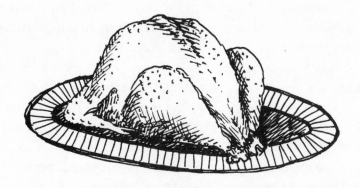

This *avgolemono* soup is popular throughout Greece, and is made with tiny meatballs. Ground lamb is usually used there, but ground beef, veal, pork, or lamb can be used alone or in any combination. We sampled bowls of this delightful soup in beautiful Nauplia, on the east coast of the Peloponesus.

Nauplia is an Italian-looking city on a wide bay. It has a magnificent main square, tiled and immaculate, which is surrounded on all sides with apartment villas, painted in varied earth tones, similar to those of Siena. We stayed in town and all was within walking distance. From our window we could see a castle on the hill behind the town.

Once we were settled, we drove a short distance to view the ancient theater at Epidauros, and later enjoyed a typical Greek dinner at one of the restaurants on the square. Ice cream cones along the waterfront promenade followed. Out in the bay lies a fortified island and we watched as floodlights came on to illuminate the old walls and towers.

Meatball and Avgolemono Soup

3/4 pound finely ground lamb, veal, beef, or pork
1 small onion, grated (catch the juice, too)
1 small clove garlic, minced
3 tablespoons raw white rice
2 tablespoons finely minced fresh parsley
1 tablespoon finely minced fresh mint
  salt and pepper to taste
3 large eggs
1 quart chicken stock
1 small onion, diced (optional)
1 small stalk celery, diced (optional)
1 small carrot, peeled and diced (optional)
  juice of 1 lemon

Mix the meat, grated onion, garlic, rice, parsley, mint, salt, pepper, and 1 egg together. Knead until the mix is smooth. Form into small meatballs, about 1 inch in diameter. Set aside.

Pour the stock into a soup pot. Add the onion, celery, and carrot if you wish vegetables in the soup. Bring to a boil, reduce to a simmer, and carefully slide the meatballs into the soup, one by one, to poach. Cover the pot and cook at a low simmer for 30 minutes.

Whisk together the remaining 2 eggs and the lemon juice. Slowly add a cup of the hot broth to the egg mix, whisking the whole time. Return all to the cooked soup, stirring constantly.

Slowly raise the heat, stirring until the soup thickens. Do not allow it to boil. Serve immediately.

Serves 4.

One more variation on the lemon and egg sauce theme in Greek soups—clearly a popular taste—is this one made with celery. We've enjoyed similar one-vegetable *avgolemono* soups, made with tomatoes or leeks. This creamy celery soup was eaten at a lunch stop we made along the east coast of southern Greece.

A small road branched off the main one, and we could see it would bring us closer to the water, which looked invitingly cool and blue in the distance. Near the edge of the road stood a restaurant with pink bougainvillaea growing over its awning-shaded terrace. Along with the soup, we had *spanakopita* (a flaky cheese and spinach pastry).

It was lovely and peaceful there, steps away from a tiny white beach—the kind of place that tempts one to abandon all else and stay forever!

Creamy Celery and Avgolemono Soup

> 1 tablespoon butter
> 1 small onion, diced
> 5 stalks celery, sliced very thin
> 1 quart chicken stock
> 2 tablespoons tiny pasta shapes (stars or orzo)
> 2 eggs
> juice of 1 lemon
> salt and pepper to taste
> 2 tablespoons finely minced parsley

In a soup pot, melt the butter and gently sauté the onion and celery for 5 minutes. Add the stock, bring to a boil, lower to a simmer, cover, and cook for 15 minutes. Add the pasta and cook for 10 more minutes.

Whisk together the eggs and the lemon juice. Slowly add 1 cup of the hot soup, whisking constantly. Return all to the soup pot. Continue stirring briskly, slowly raising the heat until the sauce thickens enough to coat the spoon. Do not let the soup boil. Add salt and pepper to taste. Serve immediately, sprinkled with fresh parsley.

Serves 4.

Variations:

Substitute 4 washed leeks, white parts only, for the celery. Slice very thin.

or

Substitute 3 peeled, seeded, diced, very ripe tomatoes for the celery.

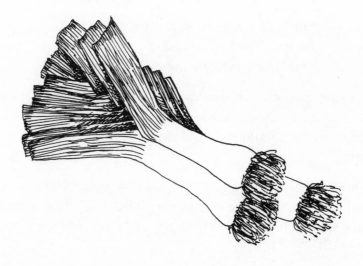

On the east coast of southern Greece, there is a medieval town called Monemvasia. We heard it described as a fortress, completely covering a small, rocky island, reachable only by a narrow bridge. As we rounded a bend on the coastal road, we could see it sitting just off shore, a walled town built long ago.

We were allowed to bring our car as far as the end of the bridge, then we walked through giant gates, and up a steep, narrow road. We only had small backpacks, but more substantial luggage, as well as everything else the town needed, was brought in by donkeys. They clip-clopped endlessly, up and down, loaded with supplies.

The one main street, really a vine-shaded path no more than fifteen feet wide, contained several small restaurants and inns. We secured a room in one that was tidy and comfortable. The back of the room was clearly built into, and was part of, the stone island. In the space of an hour it was possible to walk every inch of the town. The sea is visible from everywhere, and the restaurant we selected had three tables set up on a minuscule terrace, overlooking the water.

The meal began with a true Greek and Turkish classic—cold cucumber and yogurt soup. Both countries make this refreshing summertime treat the same way.

Cucumber and Yogurt Soup

> 1 large cucumber
> 1/4 teaspoon salt
> 1 clove garlic, minced
> 3 cups whole-milk yogurt
> 1 tablespoon olive oil
> 1 tablespoon vinegar
> 1/4 cup fresh dill, minced *or* 1/4 cup fresh mint, minced
>   pinch of cayenne pepper

Peel the cucumber and cut it lengthwise. Scoop out the seeds with a spoon. Coarsely grate the cucumber, collecting both pulp and juice in a bowl. Sprinkle with salt, mix, and let it rest for 15 minutes.

Mix the garlic, yogurt, oil, vinegar, dill or mint, and pepper in another bowl. Add the cucumber with its salty liquid. Stir. Chill for several hours.

Serves 4.

Basil, so popular in Italy, is seldom used in Greek cooking for a very interesting reason. Legend has it that pieces of the crucifixion cross of Christ were found on a basil-covered hill. Ever since, the religious Greeks have revered, rather than eaten, this special herb. Soup like this, in Italy, would almost certainly contain fresh basil. Here it is made with dill or mint.

We ate something like this one hot summer day near the ruins of Mycenae, the oldest mainland settlement in Greece. Touring the site is very strenuous, involving lots of climbing uphill over rocky, slippery paths; so this soup provided a welcome and refreshing lunch. It has an intriguing sweet-salty taste.

Cold Tomato Bean Soup

> 1/2 cup sun-dried tomatoes
> 2 tablespoons olive oil
> 2 onions, chopped
> 2 leeks, white parts only, washed and sliced thin
> 1 clove garlic, minced
> 1 14-ounce can chickpeas *or* cannellini beans, drained
> 2 14-ounce cans diced tomatoes
> 2 cups chicken stock
> 1/2 cup fresh chopped dill *or* mint
> salt and pepper to taste
> 4 tablespoons crumbled feta cheese

If the sun-dried tomatoes are hard, bring them to a boil, and let them soak in the hot water for 10 minutes. Chop them into small pieces.

In a soup pot, heat the oil and slowly sauté the onions, leeks, and garlic for 10 minutes. Do not let them brown.

Add the beans, sun-dried tomatoes, canned tomatoes, and stock. Bring to a boil, reduce to a simmer, cover, and cook for 30 minutes.

Add the dill or mint, and cook for 10 minutes. Add salt and pepper to taste.

Chill thoroughly. Serve cold the next day, sprinkled with feta cheese.

Serves 4.

The winter weather throughout Greece is cold, rainy, and gusty—
the perfect weather for a hearty soup of winter vegetables. By American standards, Mediterranean people eat very little meat, preferring
instead to get their protein from grains and legumes, seafood, and
dairy products.

Greek Winter Soup

> 1/2 cup dried chickpeas, soaked overnight
> 2 quarts beef stock
> 1 meaty ham or lamb bone (optional)
> 1 potato, peeled and diced
> 3 cloves garlic, sliced
> 1 leek, white part only, chopped
> 1 onion, chopped
> 1 rutabaga *or* turnip, peeled and diced
> 1 carrot, peeled and sliced
> 1 stalk celery, chopped
> 1/4 head Savoy cabbage, chopped
> 4 large kale leaves, chopped
> 1/2 cup barley
> 2 bay leaves
> 2 sprigs thyme
> 2 sprigs marjoram
>   salt and pepper to taste
>   olive oil (as garnish)

Bring the soaked chickpeas to a boil, remove from the heat, and allow
to sit for 1 hour. Drain.

Put all the ingredients including the chickpeas, in a large soup pot.
Bring to a boil, reduce to a simmer, cover, and cook for 1 hour, or
until the chickpeas are tender. This soup should be thick.

This soup is even better reheated the next day. If there is a soup bone,
pick off all the meat. Return the meat to the soup and discard the
bone. Serve hot, with olive oil drizzled over each portion.

Serves 6.

As one leaves Athens and the big towns behind in Greece, it becomes increasingly difficult to read directions. In the most rural areas, signs are written solely in the Cyrillic alphabet. The names of well-known places are rendered unintelligible to our western eyes. Oh, if we had only studied our Greek letters with more diligence at school those many years ago!

We were becoming more lost by the minute, as we passed through one tiny settlement after another, none of which was even big enough to merit map recognition. Two hours earlier we thought we were on the right road to reach the ancient Greek temple to Apollo at Bassae. We knew it had stood in an isolated valley for 2,500 years, and we certainly were close. Several stops were made, only to prove fruitless; no one spoke English. Oh well, it was a beautiful day, we had plenty of gas; we'd get there eventually.

One last stop for directions, this time at a farmhouse. An old farmer and his wife were sitting cross-legged on the ground in front of big pieces of burlap covered with dried figs. They were stringing them on pieces of strong, flexible vine and tying them into the familiar ovals we find wrapped in cellophane in our supermarkets.

The old couple studied our map, smiled a lot, and pointed us up the road. Then, with typical Greek hospitality, she loaded my arms and skirt with delicious dried figs before we were allowed to go. We nibbled on them for days, eventually did find Bassae, and every time we buy figs labeled Greek, we wonder if our bunch was packed by that dear old couple.

The hospitality of the Greeks seems to manifest itself in the generous sharing of food. At the moment we arrived, the old couple had nothing but their figs to give, but it is likely that a soup pot was inside, bubbling on the stove in preparation for a big family dinner. Bean soup like this, called *fassoulada,* is prepared there a million times a day. It is the Greek comfort food and symbol of their open hospitality.

Greek Bean Soup

- 1 pound dry white beans, such as navy or cannellini, soaked overnight
- 3 tablespoons olive oil
- 2 onions, chopped
- 3 cloves garlic, minced
- 2 stalks celery, chopped
- 2 carrots, peeled and sliced thin
- 1 bay leaf
- 1 teaspoon dry cumin
- 1 14-ounce can diced tomatoes
- 1/4 teaspoon hot red pepper flakes
- 2 quarts chicken stock
- 1/2 cup chopped fresh parsley
- 2 sprigs fresh thyme *or* 2 tablespoons fresh mint
  salt to taste

Optional: If you have a ham bone, you may put it in when you first start this soup cooking. If not, you may wish to drizzle some extra virgin olive oil into each portion at serving time.

Drain the soaking water off the beans.

In a soup pot, heat the oil and sauté the onions, garlic, celery, and carrots for 5 minutes. Put in the bay leaf, cumin, tomatoes, and pepper. Pour in the stock.

Add the beans (and the ham bone if you wish), bring to a boil, reduce to a simmer, and cook, covered, for 2 to 3 hours, or until the beans are tender.

Add the parsley, and thyme or mint, during the last 15 minutes.

If you are using a ham bone, remove any bits of meat from it and return the meat to the pot. Serve hot.

Serves 6 to 8.

Before Columbus and the exploration of the New World, only fava beans, lentils, and chickpeas were in cultivation around the Mediterranean. Many traditional dishes containing them have evolved. New World transplants like navy, pinto, black, and kidney beans, even to this day, are found less frequently.

Every Mediterranean country has its version of a lentil soup, using favorite seasonings to make the soup their own. Greece's lentil soup, called *faki,* is considered a Lenten dish, although it is a favorite all year. It is said that the very strictest Orthodox Christians make it without the pleasure of olive oil on Good Friday.

Greek Lentil Soup (Faki)

            2 tablespoons olive oil
            1 onion, chopped
            1 stalk celery plus leaves, chopped
            1 carrot, peeled and chopped
            2 cloves garlic, minced
            1 pound lentils
            2 quarts water *or* chicken stock
            1 14-ounce can diced tomatoes
            1 bay leaf
          1/2 cup chopped fresh parsley
          1/4 cup chopped fresh mint *or* 1 tablespoon fresh oregano
                leaves
                salt and pepper to taste
      2 or 3 tablespoons red wine vinegar

In a large soup pot, heat the oil and sauté the onion, celery, carrot, and garlic for 5 minutes.

Pour in the lentils, water or stock, tomatoes, bay leaf, parsley, and mint or oregano. Bring to a boil, reduce to a simmer, and cook, covered, for 1 hour or more, or until the lentils are very tender. This soup should be thick.

Season it with salt and pepper, and just before serving, stir in the vinegar.

Serves 6.

We never tried this odd soup in Greece, but a Greek-American friend shared this recipe. It is considered the ultimate fasting soup, even forgoing olive oil, and is served during Lent. Tahini is sesame seed paste or butter, widely available in grocery and Middle Eastern food stores. Keep it refrigerated after opening, and try to mix the oil evenly through before using.

Tahini Soup

    1¹/₂ quarts water
    ¹/₂ cup raw white rice
    ¹/₂ teaspoon salt
    ¹/₂ cup tahini
    juice of 1¹/₂ lemons (about 5 or 6 tablespoons)
    1 teaspoon tomato paste
    pepper to taste

In a soup pot, bring the water, rice, and salt to a boil. Lower to simmer, cover, and cook for 20 minutes.

In the meantime, put the tahini and about ¹/₂ cup of water in a blender. Process, then add the lemon juice, the tomato paste, pepper, and 1 or 2 cups of the hot rice water. (Without a blender, this can all be done with a wire whisk.)

Remove the rest of the rice soup from the heat, and stir in the tahini mix.

Serves 6.

Many of the culinary traditions of Turkey and Greece are the same or nearly the same. A soup served to celebrate all Turkish weddings, called wedding soup, bears comparison with this Greek soup (see page 141). It is an interesting fact that a much more complicated version of this soup is served early Easter morning, the most joyous moment of the Greek Orthodox year. One soup, two religions, two happy occasions. In both cultures, the soups fall into the broad *avgolemono* category.

Easy Mageritsa Soup

    1 meaty veal or lamb joint
    2 onions, sliced
    1 carrot, peeled and sliced
    2 stalks celery with leaves, sliced
    2 cloves garlic, sliced
  1 1/2 quarts chicken stock
   1/2 cup raw rice *or* orzo pasta
    3 eggs
      juice of 1 lemon (4 tablespoons)
      salt and pepper to taste
    2 tablespoons minced fresh parsley *or* dill

In a large soup pot, place the meat, onions, carrot, celery, garlic, and stock. Bring to a boil, reduce to a simmer, and cook, covered, for 2 1/2 hours.

Allow to cool a bit. Pick out the meat and bone. Remove the meat from the bone. Chop or shred it and set aside. Discard the bone.

Strain the rest of the soup through a fine sieve, pressing on the vegetables to extract all the flavor. Discard the vegetables in the strainer. Return the meat and soup to the pot. Add the rice or pasta. Simmer for 15 minutes.

In a meantime, whisk together the eggs and lemon juice. When the rice or pasta is tender, scoop out 1 cup of the soup, and slowly whisk it into the eggs. Return all to the pot. Slowly raise the heat, continuing to whisk, until the soup thickens. Do not let it boil. Add salt and pepper to taste.

Serve hot, sprinkled with fresh herbs.

Serves 4 to 6.

In Greece, more than in any other Mediterranean country, certain foods are inextricably linked to the religious calendar. Red-dyed eggs baked in a special bread for Easter morning, whole roast lamb on Easter evening, special fasting foods for Lent, bean soups for Fridays (always a fasting day); the list goes on.

A true classic is this complicated soup called Mageritsa, which frugally uses all the parts of the freshly killed lamb that cannot be used for roasting on Easter. It is always prepared on Holy Saturday, but can't be tasted by the housewife as it cooks, as she is still on her fast.

It is the first food that breaks the forty days of meatless Lent and it is consumed, along with red-dyed eggs, just after midnight early Easter morning, when families return from church. The next day, a great roast lamb feast is prepared.

Unlikely to be prepared as it is written here, after reading this recipe, consider preparing the Easy Mageritsa on page 125.

Traditional Mageritsa

> liver, heart, lungs, intestines (tripe), head, and feet of a lamb
>
> 2 large onions, chopped
> 1 carrot, peeled and chopped
> 2 stalks celery with leaves, chopped
> 2 cloves garlic, chopped
> 2 quarts chicken stock
> 1/2 cup raw rice *or* orzo pasta
> salt and pepper to taste
> 3 eggs
> juice of 2 lemons

In a big soup pot, place the thoroughly cleaned head, feet, intestines, and lungs of the lamb. Cover with water and bring to a boil. Cook for 1 hour. Discard the water.

In a fresh pot, place the heart, liver, vegetables, and stock. Bring to a boil, reduce to a simmer, cover, and cook for 30 minutes.

In the meantime, cut 1-inch squares of tripe and lungs, as much as you want. Put them in the soup. Crack open the head and remove the brain. Cut it into cubes. Pick the meat off the feet.

After 30 minutes, take the heart and liver out of the soup. Cut them into cubes, and add back as much as you want to the soup. Add in the reserved brain, feet meat, and the rice or orzo. Simmer for 20 minutes. Add salt and pepper to taste.

Whisk together the eggs and lemon juice. Slowly pour 1 cup of hot broth into the egg mix, continuing to whisk. Add all back into the soup. Raise the heat slowly, continuing to mix, until the soup thickens. Do not let it boil.

Serves 6 to 8.

Turkish Soups

Just as certain skyscrapers represent the skyline of Manhattan, and the Eiffel Tower can only mean Paris, so too does the famous dome and minarets of Sancta Sophia signal Istanbul. Built in 500 A.D. by Justinian, when the city was still called Constantinople, it was, and still is, an architectural wonder. First used as the Christian church of the Holy Wisdom, it was later converted to a mosque, and is now a museum. Its great dome measures over 100 feet in diameter and rises almost 200 feet from the floor, with no visible support beyond its walls.

To walk into Sancta Sophia today inspires awe; one can only imagine what was felt 1,500 years ago. Then its walls glittered with mosaics lit by the light of thousands of oil lamps and candles. Later, some of the mosaics were plastered over by the Muslims, in an effort to cover Christian images, thereby saving these exquisite examples of Byzantine art. Sancta Sophia is truly a wonder of the ancient world which has withstood wars, fires, and earthquakes, remaining miraculously intact for us to enjoy.

We had spent a long morning there, climbing to the second floor gallery, the better to appreciate the view and to get closer to some of the remaining mosaics, images we had previously seen only in art books.

Sancta Sophia is in the heart of old Istanbul. Today it is surrounded by Topkapi Palace, the Blue Mosque, the Covered Bazaar, apartments, hotels, and restaurants. Even its minarets are a new addition.

Older than Constantinople itself, are the grain soups which predate even the Greeks and Romans. They have come down to us in an unbroken line from the earliest nomadic tribes in Anatolia. Portable, frugal, nourishing—these one-pot meals sustained the earliest citizens of Turkey. Try the following two variations:

Farina Soup

1¹/₂ quarts beef stock
¹/₂ cup farina (semolina or cream of wheat)
4 tablespoons lemon juice (1 lemon)
3 eggs
salt and pepper to taste

Bring the beef stock to a boil and gradually add the farina. Boil for 3 minutes. Remove from the heat.

Beat the lemon juice and eggs together, then add to the soup. Mix constantly. Return the soup to the stove and slowly bring to a simmer. Do not boil again. Add salt and pepper.

Serve immediately.

Serves 4.

Tomato Farina Soup

    3 tablespoons butter
  1/2 cup farina (semolina or cream of wheat)
1 1/2 quarts chicken stock
    1 14-ounce can diced tomatoes
    3 eggs
  1/3 cup whole milk
     salt and pepper to taste

In a large saucepan, melt the butter and add the farina. Cook over medium heat for 5 minutes, stirring constantly.

Add the chicken stock. Bring to a boil, stirring constantly. Boil for 3 minutes.

Add the tomatoes and their juice. Reduce the heat, then simmer for 30 minutes.

In a small bowl, beat the eggs and milk together. Slowly add to the simmering soup, stirring constantly. Simmer for 3 minutes. Add salt and pepper. Serve at once.

Serves 4.

We flew from Istanbul to Trabzon, a small city at the far eastern end of the Black Sea, with the intention of renting a car and taking a week or so to drive back. There was a monastery, some old Ottoman towns, and lots of beautiful scenery to see in this rather forgotten area of Turkey. The cities of the Black Sea coast, such as Trabzon, Sinop, and Samsun, are thousands of years old, but even today there is only one winding coastal road—and much isolation.

Our first stop, after spending a day in Trabzon, was the legendary Sumela Monastery, about an hour's drive inland and an hour's climb straight up. The monks of the 14th century were looking for a quiet contemplative spot and built a tiny town clinging to a cliff. Their small cells, a chapel, and a postage stamp-sized courtyard are all that could fit there. The outside surfaces, especially of the chapel, are covered with frescos, now faint with the ages. The views of the forests and distant mountains contribute to the tranquillity. Save for a care-taker, we were alone to enjoy this serene, pious spot.

The further east one goes in Turkey, the closer one comes to the birthplace of yogurt. Yogurt began, in all probability, as the acci-dental holding of milk at a warm temperature, in the presence of the right cultures. The fermenting process creates a tangy, long-lasting product that is kind to the stomach and can serve as a drink (ayran), cheese, soup, dessert, or salad. It is even mixed with wheat, dried and formed into pellets, ready to be reconstituted in times of shortage.

Many Turkish soups are enriched with yogurt, just as they are in the Middle East. The following three soups are a representative group that we've sampled. All are quick and easy; one is served cold.

*Also see the recipe for Cottage Soup on page 136 for another yogurt-based soup.

Chicken Yogurt Soup

> 1 quart chicken stock
> 1/3 cup white rice
> 2 cups yogurt

2 eggs
  salt and pepper to taste
  fresh mint, chopped

In a soup pot, simmer the stock and rice for about 15 minutes, or until the rice is tender. Remove the pot from the heat.

Meanwhile, beat together the yogurt and eggs.

Slowly add the yogurt mix to the hot stock, stirring constantly. When all is stirred in, return the pot to the heat, stirring constantly. Do not allow it to boil. Add salt and pepper.

Serve immediately in individual bowls. Pass chopped mint as a garnish.

Serves 4.

Beef Yogurt Soup

1 quart beef stock
2 cups yogurt
  salt and pepper to taste
4 tablespoons butter
4 tablespoons flour
1/2 clove garlic, minced
  fresh mint, chopped

Mix the beef stock, yogurt, salt, and pepper together in a bowl.

In a soup pot, melt the butter, then add the flour and garlic. Cook for several minutes.

With the heat on high, slowly add the beef broth mix, stirring constantly until all comes to a boil. Cook the thickened mix for several minutes.

Serve hot in individual bowls. Pass fresh mint as a garnish.

Serves 4.

Cold Tomato Soup

    1 cup yogurt
    3 cups canned tomato juice
    1 tablespoon olive oil
    2 tablespoons lemon juice
    2 tablespoons white vinegar
    1/2 teaspoon curry powder
      salt to taste
    1 lemon, sliced wafer thin
      fresh parsley, minced

In a large bowl, stir the yogurt until smooth. Using a wire whisk, beat in the tomato juice, olive oil, lemon juice, vinegar, and curry powder. Taste and add salt if desired.

Chill for several hours.

Ladle into chilled bowls, float a lemon slice on each, and sprinkle with parsley.

Serves 4.

Cappadocia, in central Turkey, is one of the oddest inhabited spots in the world. Millions of years ago, volcanoes poured lava over hundreds of square miles in the center of Turkey. It settled to form high plateaus of ash and mud, which eroded over time into a fantastic moonscape of deep ravines and tall cones.

Four thousand years ago the Hittites discovered it could be easily carved into dwellings, the surface hardening upon contact with air. Ever since, groups of people have called it "home." Each successive group added to the collection of churches, stables, and houses to create whole towns of cave-like structures carved into the hills and mountains.

In 700 A.D., to escape the advancing armies of Islam, Christians in Cappadocia hid their towns underground. Eight stories deep, and home to 60,000, they are quite astonishing to explore. Like gigantic rock sponges, sloping passageways lead from room to room. Nothing showing on the surface, thousands of people lived for years, hidden from their enemies.

The entire region lies along caravan routes which, in another era, were criss-crossed by long processions of camels and men, bringing trade goods east and west. Nomadic tribes also have called hot, dry Cappadocia home.

The earliest foods of all these people consisted of one-pot soups and stews of grains, and fermented milk from their animals. Food historians feel that yogurt was first discovered as it formed in bladders of milk riding on the warm flanks of draft animals—a fortunate mistake!

This grain and yogurt soup originated in eastern Turkey, where the Kurdish people still prepare it today. Notice that it is made with butter, rather than olive oil. Nomadic people have access to butter from their animals, but plant no olive trees.

Cottage Soup

>   1 large onion, minced
>   3 tablespoons butter
>   2/3 cup uncooked barley
>   2 quarts beef stock
>   3 cups yogurt
>   5 tablespoons flour
>   2 eggs
>   1 cup water
>   1/2 cup minced mint *or* parsley *or* cilantro
>   salt and pepper to taste
>   4 tablespoons butter
>   3/4 teaspoon cayenne pepper

In a soup pot, sauté the onion in the 3 tablespoons of butter for 5 minutes. Add the barley, then sauté for 1 minute more.

Add the stock and simmer until the barley is just tender (about 30 minutes).

In a bowl, beat together the yogurt, flour, eggs, and water. Slowly add to the simmering soup, stirring constantly until the soup is thickened. Cover and simmer for 10 minutes.

Add the mint or parsley or cilantro, then simmer for 3 minutes more. Add salt and pepper to taste.

In a small pot, melt the 4 tablespoons of butter and add the cayenne pepper.

Serve the soup hot and allow each person to add a spoon or two of the butter-pepper mix to their soup.

Serves 6 to 8.

Every culture, every cuisine has its version of vegetable soup. Many soups in Turkey include dairy products, especially yogurt, but this one is enriched with cream.

Creamy Vegetable Soup

    2 tablespoons butter
    1 onion, minced
    2 green peppers, diced
    1 14-ounce can diced tomatoes
    1 quart chicken stock
    1/4 cup white rice
    3/4 cup whole milk
    1/4 cup heavy cream
        salt and pepper to taste
    1/2 cup minced parsley
    4 slices white bread, cut in 1/2-inch cubes

In a soup pot, melt the butter and sauté the onions and peppers for 5 minutes. Add the tomatoes with their juice, the chicken stock, rice, milk, cream, salt, and pepper.

Simmer for 30 minutes. Add parsley the last 5 minutes.

In the meantime, spread the bread cubes on an oven tray. Toast in a 400° oven, turning frequently, until golden brown.

Serve with toasted bread cubes on top.

Serves 4 to 6.

On four occasions, we've been lucky enough to spend some days in the great and historic city of Istanbul. Each time, we've seen new 20th-century changes; the charming old floating bridge across the Golden Horn has been replaced, public transportation has improved, and the picturesque drinking-water vendors have all but disappeared. What we fondly remember from our earliest visits were great markets, a colorful and chaotic waterfront, and one tiny door on a side street that we almost missed.

An old sign there, in several languages, reads "Roman Cistern." For a small fee we entered and descended into a cavernous and dim netherworld. Roman style arches, supported by a forest of columns, held up the roof. Each of the hundreds of columns, stretching as far as we could see into the distance, rested in an absolutely still black lake. A few discreet lights showed the way along catwalks suspended above the water. We were in the main reservoir for Roman Constantinople, built by Justinian to supply water for the city. How eerily fascinating! Years later, on another visit, we noticed it had become a major tourist attraction.

On the same street as the Roman Cistern, there is a small outdoor cafe that we had been to before. They make a wonderful lentil soup that is done in the traditional Turkish style. Every Mediterranean country has its version of lentil soup. Lentils have been in cultivation there for over 2,000 years, one of the legumes indigenous to Europe and the Middle East.

You may have to hunt a bit for red lentils. Regular brown lentils taste the same and are fine, but nothing can substitute for the beautiful, rich, orange color of the soup when made the Turkish way, with red lentils. It is a hearty and nutritious winter soup and a particular favorite of ours.

Red Lentil Soup

    2 cups red lentils
    6 tablespoons butter
    1 large onion, chopped
    4 cups water
    2 tablespoons flour
    1 quart beef stock
    2 eggs
    1 cup milk
    salt and cayenne pepper to taste
4 or 5 slices day-old French or Italian bread
    fresh parsley, chopped
    fresh mint, chopped

Wash and pick over the lentils. In a soup pot, melt 2 tablespoons of the butter and lightly brown the onion. Add the water and lentils. Bring to a boil, reduce heat, and simmer for 30 to 40 minutes, or until the lentils are quite soft. Allow to cool slightly.

In a small saucepan, melt 2 more tablespoons of butter, add the flour, and allow to foam and cook together for 1 minute. Slowly add in 1 cup of the stock, stirring constantly over heat until the mixture thickens.

In a blender or food processor, purée the lentil and water mix until smooth. Return to the large pot, add the remaining 3 cups of stock, and bring to a boil.

Slowly add in the flour and stock mix from the small pot, stirring well. Reduce heat and simmer for 5 minutes.

Beat the eggs and milk together well. Slowly add to the hot soup. Heat, but do not allow it to boil again.

Add salt and cayenne pepper to taste.

To make croutons: Cut the bread into ½-inch cubes. Melt the last 2 tablespoons of butter in a skillet and fry the breadcrumbs on all sides until golden.

Serve the soup hot. Pass garnishes of croutons, parsley, and mint for each person to add as desired.

Serves 8.

Served at all weddings and other joyous events in Turkey, this soup is similar to the Greek Mageritsa Soup on page 125. It is perfect as a first course, or for lunch.

Wedding Soup

> 1 pound lamb pieces, trimmed of fat
> 1 carrot, peeled and sliced
> 1 onion, quartered
> 6 cups water
>   salt and pepper to taste
> 6 tablespoons butter
> 1/2 cup flour
> 4 tablespoons lemon juice (1 lemon)
> 3 egg yolks

garnish:

> 3 tablespoons butter
> 1 tablespoon paprika
> 1/8 teaspoon cayenne pepper

In a large saucepot, combine the lamb, carrot, onion, water, salt, and pepper.

Bring to a boil, cover, and simmer for 1 1/2 hours, or until the lamb is quite tender.

Cool a bit; strain off the meat and vegetables and save the soup. Shred the lamb and discard the vegetables.

In a separate saucepan, melt the 6 tablespoons of butter and add the flour. Stir and cook for several minutes, then slowly add the soup, whisking constantly until bubbling and smooth.

Add the meat shreds and simmer for 10 minutes.

Beat the lemon juice and egg yolks together in a bowl. Stir in a cup of the hot soup, then slowly added all to the soup pot, whisking well.

Heat but do not allow it to boil.

In a small pot, melt the butter for the garnish. Stir in the paprika and cayenne pepper.

Serve individual hot bowls of soup. Pass the melted butter mix so that each person may add a spoon of it to their soup.

Serves 6 to 8.

Anatolia, the land that we call Turkey today, has played host to Lycians, Greeks, Romans, and many other people over the millennia. It is the Greek and Roman cities whose histories have created the most fascinating sites to visit today. Everywhere, from the center of Anatolia on, to the west and south, dozens of the remains of these great settlements can be explored. There is the familiar Ephesus on the west coast, dramatic Pergamum to the north, Aphrodisias with its famed ancient school of sculpture, and the less visited sites of Side, Aspendos, and Perge in the south.

We have no favorite; each has its own unique quality. What is certain, though, is that the Greeks and Romans were masterful builders of temples, theaters, roads, baths, meeting halls, and aqueducts. Their 2,000-year-old architectural idioms come down to us today, still appropriate for great structures. Museums all over the world are crammed full of their vases, sculpture, and artifacts. And nowhere is the quest to see all this more accessible than in Turkey.

Also coming down to us from Greek, Roman, and later times are bean and meat stews (although poor people in any age seldom ate meat, subsisting instead on beans, grains, and field herbs). This hearty stew contains New World tomatoes, and dates from Ottoman times. It is called Janissary Stew after the sultan's own soldiers.

Janissary Stew

> 4 tablespoons butter
> 1½ pounds boneless lean lamb, cut into ¾ inch cubes
> 2 medium onions, chopped
> 2 14-ounce cans diced tomatoes
> 3 cups beef stock
> ¼ teaspoon cayenne pepper or more
>   salt to taste
> 2 14-ounce cans great northern beans, drained

In a soup pot, melt the butter, then slowly sauté the meat and onion until browned.

Add the tomatoes, stock, pepper, and salt. Lower heat to a simmer, cover, and cook for 1 hour.

Add the beans, mix well, and simmer for 15 minutes.

Serve hot with a green salad and bread.

Serves 4.

Birdseed vendor, Istanbul, Turkey

Istanbul is a city divided into three parts by water. To the south of the Golden Horn, which is an estuary off the Bosporus, lies the old city. Here one can explore ancient mosques and markets, Sancta Sophia, and Topkapi Palace. To the east, across the Bosporus, lie the Asian suburbs of Istanbul. From there, small towns are connected by fast ferries to the city. To the north, across the Golden Horn, are the commercial areas. Lining its broad boulevards are banks, businesses, restaurants, and the biggest hotels.

We wandered along a traffic-free avenue of fine shops and foreign embassies there. Our goal for dinner was a side street containing many small restaurants, known as the Flower Passage. In the restaurant we chose, it seemed that everyone was ordering a particular soup. We gave it a try. It turned out to be tripe soup. We learned later that it is considered to be a cure for hangovers. It was surprisingly good, especially with its spicy and garlicky additions.

Turkish "Hangover" Soup

> 3 pounds tripe, thoroughly washed
> 2 quarts water
> salt and pepper to taste
> 6 tablespoons butter
> 6 tablespoons flour
> 2 eggs
> 8 tablespoons lemon juice (2 lemons)
> 2 tablespoons butter
> 1/2 teaspoon cayenne pepper
> 6 tablespoons vinegar
> 4 tablespoons garlic, minced

Place the tripe in a soup pot with the water. Simmer covered for 1 hour. Drain. Save the liquid. Chop the tripe into small pieces. Return to the liquid and add salt and pepper. Cook until the tripe is tender, about another hour or more. It will dissolve if cooked too long.

In a small pot, melt the butter and add the flour. Cook for 2 minutes, until bubbly. Ladle 2 cups of the soup into the flour mix. Whisk over heat, until thick and smooth. Return it to the soup pot to thicken the soup. Simmer for 10 minutes.

In a separate bowl, beat the eggs and lemon juice together and slowly add to the simmering soup, stirring constantly. At this point check the seasoning, then add more water if the soup is too thick.

In a small pot, heat the butter and pepper together. In a small bowl, mix the vinegar and garlic together. Serve the soup hot, with a bit of the pepper-butter over each serving. Pass the garlic-vinegar to be added by each person.

Serves 6 to 8.

Without doubt, one of the most fascinating sights in Turkey, one of its great natural wonders, is the hot springs at Pamukkale. From a distance, it seems to be a single small snow-covered mountain, but as one drives closer it becomes clear that the mountain is covered in white mineral deposits.

We drove up a winding road to the top and found ourselves in a kind of resort with several hotels, restaurants, and a museum. We were in the ancient Roman spa of Hierapolis, refitted for modern travelers. Our hotel was built partially within the walls of an 11th-century Byzantine castle. Its pool's edge had been raised to catch the warm, slightly effervescent water flowing out of the mountain. Below our pool were banks of naturally occurring smaller pools looking like pure-white, terraced, rice paddies. Hundreds were playing or soaking in the calcium-rich water, just as people have been doing for 2,000 years.

The sunset that night was magnificent—a bright orange ball dropping through a cloudless sky. From our table at a terrace restaurant, we watched people splashing in the shallow terraces until well after dark.

Our meal began with a choice of soups. We passed up the cucumber-yogurt and the chicken avgolemono soups, both of which we had tried many times, deciding instead on a borscht-like soup tinted a deep rose from the beets it contained. It was enriched with yogurt, and ours was served ice cold; but at other times we've had similar soups served hot.

Turkish Vegetable Soup

2 tablespoons butter
2 stalks celery, cut in pieces
2 carrots, peeled, and cut in pieces
2 cloves garlic, minced
2 onions, chopped
6 cups beef stock
2 medium potatoes, peeled and cut in pieces
1 sweet red pepper, seeded and chopped
2 ripe tomatoes, chopped
1/4 head cabbage, chopped
3 beet roots, scrubbed
1 bay leaf
2 cups yogurt
2 tablespoons lemon juice
  salt and pepper to taste
1 tablespoon fresh dill, minced
  fresh parsley, minced

In a large soup pot, melt the butter and sauté the celery, carrots, garlic, and onions for 4 minutes.

Pour in the stock, then add potatoes, pepper, tomatoes, cabbage, beets, and bay leaf.

Bring to a boil and reduce to a simmer. Cover and cook for 1 hour, or until the beets are tender. Take off the heat and allow to cool.

Remove the bay leaf and discard. Remove the 3 beets. When able to handle them, slip their skins off. Cut up the beets and return to the soup.

In a blender or food processor, purée the soup in batches until smooth.

With a wire whisk, add 1½ cups of the yogurt, the lemon juice, salt, pepper, and dill.

Serve hot; or chill thoroughly overnight and serve cold. Either way, place a dollop of the remaining yogurt, and a sprinkle of parsley on the soup in each individual bowl.

Serves 8.

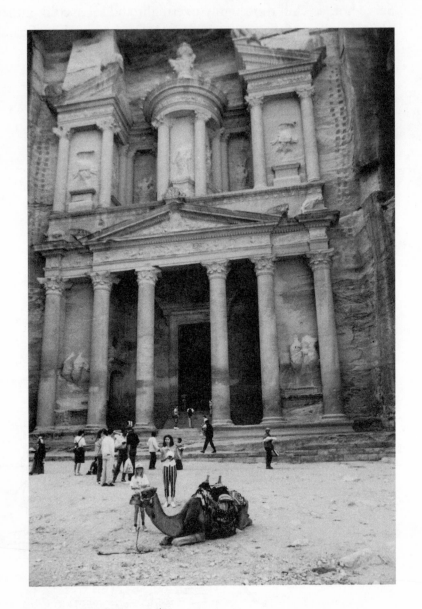

Petra, Jordan

The Middle East—Soups of Syria, Lebanon, and Jordan

● ●

The lands we call the Middle East are the ancient areas of Mesopotamia and the Levant. Today, the countries of the Syria, Lebanon, and Israel crowd the eastern shores of the Mediterranean. Parts of Turkey and Egypt are sometimes also considered part of the Middle East, but we will concentrate mostly on the soups of Syria, Lebanon, and Jordan in this section.

As every schoolchild knows, this is the part of the world where, thousands of years ago, crops were first cultivated. Archaeologists believe that the climate was simply too hostile for food gathering and hunting. People were probably forced into domesticating animals and plants and settling along rivers and oasis.

Just as old as the domestication of sheep, goats, and cows, is the culturing and fermenting of their milk to make cheese and yogurt. With this skill, early people had a product that would not spoil, and could be condensed for easy transportation. The first semi-nomadic tribes of the Middle East found this to be very useful!

The earliest domesticated crop was wheat, grown by man for at least 6,000 years. Originally an indigenous grain, early farmers learned how to grow it on irrigated land. They began to use it as a whole grain, ground it into flour, and cracked it into *burghul* (bulgur) for use in soups, salads, pilavs, and *kibbeh*.

These two early foods, yogurt and wheat, combine in a product called *kiskh*, which has been made for thousands of years as a nearly perfect food. To make kiskh, housewives boil and ferment wheat,

● ●

then dry it and grind it into fine burghul. They mix this with yogurt to make a paste. It is spread thinly on trays in the sun, then when it is dry, it is broken or ground further for easy storage. This rice or powder-like meal is stirred into soups and stews.

Today the Middle East supports a wealth of vegetables, fruits, legumes, grains, and herbs. Syria and Lebanon cultivate olives for oil, but also use butter from their animals. Their diet, day to day, does not contain much meat or fish, although sheep, goats, and chickens are the most common domesticated animals. Even though there are many Christians throughout the area, pork products are not found in their cuisines.

Many of the foods, herbs, and spices native to the Middle East were carried west by the armies of Islam into Spain, North Africa, and Sicily. Allspice, cumin, peppercorns, saffron, cinnamon, cardamon, coriander, mint, dill, pomegranate, and tahini (sesame seed paste) are a few of the aromatics carried west 1,400 years ago. These transplants still remain important tastes and smells in their native lands. All of them, plus lamb, kiskh, chickpeas, fava beans, lentils, garlic, onions, wheat berries, and barley figure heavily in their soups.

Traveling in the Middle East, for westerners, is an eye-opening experience. There is a kind of magic that is felt from the first moment. Everything is different. The smells of spices, sweets, and herbs in the marketplace, the conservatively dressed men and women, the architecture, the mosques filling with worshipers five times a day, the cries of the muezzins from the minarets, and the interesting tastes of their cuisine are all part of the magic.

The best place to sample the soups of the Middle East is in a private home. They are most often prepared in the cold winter months and to break the daily fasts of the holy month of Ramadan. If you are not lucky enough to try a home-cooked soup, the smaller restaurants, rather than fancy hotel restaurants, serve something very close to it.

It is often said that 2,000 years ago the Mediterranean was a Roman lake. Nowhere is that more evident than in the ruins of the great Roman cities of the Middle East, such as Palmyra and Jeresh.

Jeresh, in northern Jordan, is quite beautiful with its hundreds of columns, magnificent forum, impressive mosaics and carved details, broad avenues, and enormous triumphal arch built by Emperor Hadrian. Our friend Faysel drove with us to visit the ancient Roman city. We wandered, virtually alone, for several hours, taking photos and marveling, as we always do, at the genius of the Roman engineers and architects. They truly built for the ages.

Once again, when it came time to eat, we asked to go to a restaurant that served the most typical and authentic food. We began with small bowls of this soup, followed by roasted chicken smothered in sautéed onions, and covered with the thinnest leaves of the local bread.

The distinctive greens used in this soup are called *molokhia* (sometimes spelled "mlookhiyah"). They grow wild, and have been gathered for centuries for home use. I have no trouble buying frozen *molokhia* at my local Middle Eastern grocer.

Molokhia Soup

> 1 pound frozen molokhia
> 2 tablespoons butter
> 1 onion, finely chopped
> 2 cloves garlic, minced
> 1/3 cup fresh cilantro, chopped
> 1 teaspoon ground cumin
> 1 1/2 quarts chicken stock
>   salt and pepper to taste

Thaw the *molokhia* and chop very fine, or purée in a food processor.

In a soup pot, melt the butter and sauté the onion and garlic for 3 minutes.

Add the *molokhia,* cilantro, and cumin. Pour in the stock. Raise the heat to a boil, lower to a simmer, and cook, covered, for 15 minutes. Add salt and pepper to taste. Serve hot.

Serves 6.

Spice market, Syria

Throughout the Mediterranean there is a very ancient and powerful fear of the "evil eye." Italians, Turks, Greeks, the Berbers of North Africa, Syrians, Lebanese, and others believe that it is possible to cast a malevolent spell on another person. Sometimes the senders do not even realize what they are doing, sort of the Typhoid Marys of the Mediterranean. Each culture knows the indicators and how best to remove the evil.

All over Turkey blue beads or blue glass "eyes" are carried to offer protection from the evil eye. Syrians and Lebanese always know someone who can, through prayers, remove spells. Greeks and Italians carry red talismen against the evil.

My Italian great-grandmother watched us children carefully for signs of undue yawning. At this first indication that we had been "overlooked," usually by someone paying an insincere compliment about our health, good looks, or manners, she would fly into action. Special prayers were offered as she kneaded our stomachs. We were invariably cured.

As ancient as the evil eye, this chickpea and burghul (bulgur) soup is a meal in itself. Buy the wheat berries and burghul in a Middle Eastern grocery.

Thick Chickpea Soup

 1 cup dried chickpeas, soaked overnight
 1/2 cup wheat berries (jareesh), soaked overnight
 3 tablespoons olive oil
 1 large onion, chopped
 2 cloves garlic, minced
 1/2 cup medium burghul (bulgur or cracked wheat)
 11/2 quarts beef stock
 1/2 small head cabbage, shredded
 1 teaspoon paprika
 1 teaspoon ground cumin
 1/2 teaspoon allspice

$^1/_2$ teaspoon cinnamon
    salt and pepper to taste

Drain the chickpeas and wheat berries. Set aside.

In a soup pot, heat the oil and sauté the onion and garlic until slightly browned.

Add the burghul, stock, cabbage, and all the spices. Put the chickpeas and wheat berries into the pot. Raise the heat to a boil, lower to a simmer, cover, and cook until the chickpeas are tender, about $1^1/_2$ hours.

Add salt and pepper to taste. Serve hot.

Serves 6.

The following two recipes were shared with us by a Lebanese-American friend, Bob Zogby. They are traditional Lebanese and Syrian dishes, brought here by his grandmother ("sitto") and grandfather ("jitto") over 80 years ago.

To begin the first soup you will need to make one recipe of *kibbeh*. For the second soup, you will need to buy some *kiskh*. It is readily available for purchase in Middle Eastern grocery stores in major cities. Its taste is quite pleasing, some would say addictive, and is definitely worth a try. Kiskh keeps well when wrapped tightly and refrigerated.

An almost identical kibbeh soup recipe was also given to me by a Syrian-American friend, Ann Nassour.

Yogurt Soup with Kibbeh (Laban Neehee)

          kibbeh, page 245
      4 tablespoons butter
  1 1/2 cups onion, minced
      1 clove garlic, minced
    2/3 cup raw rice
      1 quart chicken stock
      1 2-inch cinnamon stick
         salt and pepper to taste
    1/4 teaspoon ground allspice
      2 tablespoons cornstarch
      5 cups full-fat yogurt
    2/3 cup fresh parsley, minced

Roll 1/2 of the kibbeh recipe into walnut-sized meatballs. (Freeze the rest for another use). Refrigerate for 1 hour. Then, in a skillet, melt 2 tablespoons of the butter and slowly brown the meatballs.

In a soup pot, melt the other 2 tablespoons of butter and slowly sauté the onions and garlic. Put the rice, stock, cinnamon, salt, pepper, and allspice in the pot. Bring to a boil and lower to a simmer.

Whisk the cornstarch into the yogurt, then add to the soup. Mix continually and slowly raise the heat until all is simmering again. Slide the meatballs into the soup, then continue to cook for about 20 minutes, or until the rice is tender.

Add the parsley. Remove the cinnamon stick. Serve hot.

Serves 6 to 8.

Crac des Chevaliers, Syria

This is the second recipe from Bob Zogby's grandmother, just as he gave it to me. Following it are some other variations of kiskh soup.

"Sitto's" Kiskh Soup

1/3 cup olive oil
1 cup minced onions
1 cup pine nuts
1 cup kiskh, see page 157
1 quart chicken stock
   salt and pepper to taste
1/8 teaspoon ground cloves
2 hard-boiled eggs, finely chopped
1/4 cup fresh parsley, minced

In a soup pot, heat the oil, and slowly sauté the onions and pine nuts. Add the kiskh and stir in the oil for 1 minute.

Slowly whisk in the stock until it comes to a boil. It should be smooth. Add the salt, pepper, and cloves. Heat and mix for several minutes.

Serve with chopped eggs and parsley on top of each bowl.

Serves 4.

The combination of dairy, especially yogurt, and a grain, most often wheat, is a strong theme in the soups of the Middle East. Nutritious, finely ground kiskh acts as a thickener and flavor enhancer to an endless variety of soups. Its taste is addictive. The following recipe uses kiskh, which, along with pomegranate syrup, is available in Middle Eastern groceries.

Lamb and Kiskh Soup

        2 tablespoons olive oil
        2 cloves garlic, minced
        1 pound lamb pieces, plus bones
        1 14-ounce can diced tomatoes
        1 quart chicken stock
        2 cups chopped greens (escarole, spinach, or romaine)
      1/8 teaspoon hot red pepper flakes
          salt to taste
        1 can cannellini, fava, or navy beans
        4 tablespoons kiskh, or more to taste (see page 157)
        2 tablespoons pomegranate syrup (also called
          pomegranate molasses)

In a soup pot, heat the oil and sauté the garlic and lamb for several minutes.

Pour in the tomatoes, stock, greens, hot pepper, and salt. Bring to a boil, lower to a simmer, cover, and cook for 1 hour, or until the lamb is tender.

Pick out the lamb bones and pull off any remaining meat. Return the meat to the soup and discard the bones.

Add the beans to the pot. Slowly mix in the kiskh, until it all dissolves and thickens the soup. Stir in the pomegranate syrup.

Simmer, uncovered, for another 10 minutes, stirring occasionally. Serve hot.

Serves 4.

If you are not yet hooked on the flavor of kiskh (be sure to only buy it fresh and refrigerated), try this last recipe, with its intriguing flavors.

Cabbage Kiskh Soup

   3 tablespoons butter
10 cloves garlic, left whole
   1 onion, chopped
   1 quart chicken stock
1/2 small cabbage, shredded
2/3 cup fresh cilantro, minced
   1 cup kiskh, see page 157
   1 tablespoon fresh mint leaves, minced
     salt and pepper to taste

In a soup pot, heat the butter and sauté the garlic and onion for 5 minutes.

Pour in the stock and cabbage. Bring to a boil, lower to a simmer, cover, and cook for 20 minutes.

Add the cilantro. Then slowly add the kiskh, mixing constantly. Bring back to a simmer, then cook for 10 minutes.

Add the mint, salt, and pepper. Let the soup rest for 10 minutes.

Serve hot.

Serves 4.

We hired a driver in Aleppo, in northern Syria, to take us on a tour of the Dead Cities, a series of ancient ghost towns—sites impossible to reach without a knowledgeable guide and his car. The roads are unmarked and often rough, and there is no bus service. Although there are hundreds of these abandoned villages in the area, we chose the six considered the best. They are remarkably well-preserved Byzantine era ruins—houses, mausoleums, temples, and public buildings—some overgrown, some barren and windswept. One, in particular, we remember well.

We were walking in from the road, toward the distant ruins, when a quite vicious dog bounded out at us. A Bedouin woman emerged from nowhere, quieted him with a well-aimed stone, then invited us to see her dwelling and the simple shelter for her animals. Built of mud brick and incorporating existing 1,500-year-old walls and columns, the total effect of the buildings and their inhabitants, out in the remote desert, was startling. With typical Bedouin hospitality, she offered us fresh milk from her goat. In return, I left her a gift of my hair barrettes.

Much later in the day we returned to Aleppo, where we were staying at the famous Baron Hotel, a vintage seen-better-days establishment of 1920s charm, which has hosted Lawrence of Arabia, Teddy Roosevelt, and Agatha Christie. It sits just outside the old city with its intriguing souks.

After a rest, we ate dinner in a charming restaurant in a restored home. It began with this soup. Nourishing soups containing dairy and grain are especially prevalent in the Middle East. In addition to kiskh soups (pages 159, 160, and 161), the two soups that follow also include grain plus dairy.

Cold Buttermilk Soup

  1/2 cup pearl barley
   salt
  1/3 cup very finely diced onion
   1 quart cultured buttermilk (you can use yogurt instead)
  1/4 teaspoon ground turmeric
  1/3 cup fresh parsley, minced
   2 tablespoons fresh dill, minced *or* 2 tablespoons fresh
    cilantro, minced
    salt and freshly ground black pepper to taste
   2 tablespoons fresh chives, minced

Cook the barley, covered, in salted water for 45 minutes. Drain and mix immediately with the onion. Cover the bowl to let the onion "cook" with the hot barley for 10 minutes.

Pour the buttermilk into the barley and onion mix. Add the turmeric, parsley, dill or cilantro, salt, and pepper.

Cover, and chill for several hours or overnight. Serve cold sprinkled with chives.

Serves 4.

One last soup worth mentioning, along the dairy-grain theme, is this yogurt and rice soup. See pages 159, 160, 161, and 163 for the other recipes. Yogurt is called laban in Syria, Lebanon, and Jordan.

Garlicky Yogurt Rice Soup

1 tablespoon butter
5 cloves garlic, minced
1/2 cup raw rice
2 cups chicken stock
3 cups full-fat yogurt (laban)
1 tablespoon cornstarch
salt and pepper to taste
2 tablespoons fresh mint leaves, minced
1 clove garlic, minced very fine

In a soup pot, heat the butter and slowly sauté the 5 cloves of garlic for 3 minutes. Add the rice, and mix over the heat for 1 minute.

Pour in the stock, bring to a boil, lower the heat to a simmer, cover, and cook for 15 minutes.

Mix the yogurt well with the cornstarch. Add to the cooked rice soup, then heat slowly, stirring constantly, until the yogurt is thickened and smooth. Add salt and pepper. If the soup is too thick, add a bit of milk, stock, or water.

Mix and macerate the mint and garlic together. Add to the soup. Simmer for 5 minutes. Serve hot.

Serves 4.

This slightly tart soup recipe comes from Ann Nassour, a Syrian-American friend. It is absolutely delicious! You will need to make one kibbeh recipe (page 245) and go to your local Middle Eastern grocer for a bottle of pomegranate syrup (also known as pomegranate molasses). The syrup keeps in the refrigerator "forever," and is used frequently in Middle Eastern soups.

Kibbeh and Carrot Soup

      1/2 kibbeh recipe, page 245, (freeze the other half for
          another use)
        2 tablespoons butter
        4 cloves garlic, minced
        6 medium carrots, peeled and sliced thin
    1 1/2 quarts beef stock
      1/2 teaspoon ground allspice
        3 tablespoons pomegranate syrup
        2 tablespoons fresh mint leaves, minced
          salt and pepper to taste

Roll the kibbeh into small, hazelnut-sized meatballs.

Heat the butter in a soup pot. Sauté the garlic and carrots for 5 minutes.

Pour in the stock, allspice, and pomegranate syrup.

Bring to a boil and reduce to a simmer.

Carefully slip the meatballs into the simmering stock and gently poach them and the carrots for 30 minutes.

Stir in the mint, salt, and pepper. Serve hot.

Serves 6.

Palmyra is one of the most famous Roman cities in the Mediterranean. We have visited many that are more complete, or more beautiful, but Palmyra's location sets it apart.

We took the excellent public bus from Damascus early one morning and traveled for several hours straight out into the desert. Minutes after leaving the city behind there is little traffic, and little to see except the sheep and tents of the Bedouin. Everything is the same beige color, until finally, in the distance, you first spot the green oasis that is Palmyra.

First mentioned in records from 4,000 years ago, it served as a way-station and staging area for countless caravans bringing goods east and west. It was the Romans who constructed the city we see today. It could only exist to begin with because of a spring that has always fed the oasis.

From the fourth floor of our hotel we could see the perfect green oval, covering many acres and surrounded by mud brick walls. Date palms alternate with olive trees, and every inch of ground beneath them is irrigated, to grow the fruits and vegetables needed for everyday use. Over the centuries, the walls have been heightened, as desert sand drifts against them. The effect is an oasis that is several yards below ground level, invitingly cool and shady in contrast with the searing desert heat.

The ruins of ancient Palmyra lie completely outside the oasis, just as the small modern tourist village does today. The oasis, then as now, serves as a huge garden to supply the town. We waited until late afternoon to visit the ruins, both to avoid the heat and to see the stately columns at sunset.

Later that evening, we tried one of the several restaurants that cater to tourists on the one main street in town and ate a surprisingly good melon soup. Winter squash or pumpkin is an often-used soup vegetable in Syria, Jordan, and Lebanon. It is sometimes combined with pieces of lamb, but is just as likely to contain no meat.

Pumpkin Soup

> 2 tablespoons butter
> 1 onion, chopped
> 1/2 pound fatless lamb cubes (optional)
> 4 cups orange winter squash pieces (pumpkin or butternut)
> 1 quart chicken stock
> salt and pepper to taste
> 1/2 teaspoon cumin
> 1/2 cup fresh mint, chopped (use with lamb) *or* 1/2 cup fresh cilantro, chopped (use without lamb)
> 1 cup full-fat yogurt

In a soup pot, heat the butter and sauté the onion. If you are using the lamb, brown it along with the onion.

Add the squash, stock, salt, pepper, and cumin.

Bring to a boil, lower to a simmer, cover, and cook for 45 minutes, or until all is tender.

Pick out the lamb pieces, then mash or purée the squash pieces. Return the meat to the soup.

Add mint if you are using lamb or cilantro if there is no lamb. Simmer for 10 minutes.

Stir in the yogurt. Serve hot.

Serves 4.

Beans of all varieties are greatly loved in the Middle East, forming a staple of their diet. They are used in appetizers, main dishes, and soups, with favorite varieties being lentils, chickpeas, fava, and white beans. Throughout the Mediterranean, for thousands of years, people have been relying on legumes and grains, often mixed with dairy products, for their protein.

Lentils are the most often-used soup legumes. This first recipe comes from a Syrian-American friend, Ann Nassour. It is her family's favorite version of lentil soup, but there are many, so I've included a variation.

Ann Nassour's Lentil Soup

    1 large onion, cut in thin slices
    2 tablespoons olive oil
    1 cup dry red lentils
  1 1/2 quarts chicken stock
  2/3 cup dry small pasta, preferably orzo
       salt and pepper to taste
   1/2 cup fresh mint leaves, minced

Sauté the onion in oil until browned. Set aside.

In a soup pot, put the lentils in the stock. Bring to a boil, lower to a simmer, and cook, covered, until the lentils are nearly cooked, about 45 minutes.

Stir in the pasta and reserved onions and cook for 10 minutes more. Add the salt, pepper, and mint. Allow the soup to rest for 10 minutes. Serve hot.

Serves 4 to 6.

Lentil soup recipes abound in the Middle East. What they seem to have in common is the use of red lentils, rice, pasta, other legumes, lots of onions and garlic, often other vegetables such as celery, tomatoes, carrots, and greens, a certain peppery-ness, and flavors such as mint, cilantro, cumin, turmeric, saffron, and pomegranate syrup or lemon. We tasted a complex soup such as this in Damascus.

Spicy Lentil Soup

3 tablespoons butter
4 cloves garlic, minced
2 onions, chopped
2 stalks celery with leaves, chopped
2 carrots, peeled and sliced thin
1 14-ounce can diced tomatoes
2 cups red lentils
2 quarts chicken stock
2 cups greens, such as spinach, chard, or escarole; chopped
1/2 teaspoon hot red pepper flakes (or more to taste)
   salt to taste
1/2 teaspoon turmeric
1 teaspoon cumin
1/2 cup raw white rice
1/2 teaspoon saffron threads
3 tablespoons lemon juice
1/2 cup fresh mint *or* cilantro, minced

In a soup pot, melt the butter and sauté the garlic, onions, celery, and carrots for 8 minutes.

Add the tomatoes, lentils, stock, greens, hot pepper, salt, turmeric, and cumin. Bring to a boil, reduce to a simmer, cover, and cook for 40 minutes. Add the rice. Cover and cook for 20 minutes, or until the lentils are very tender.

Add the saffron, lemon juice, and the mint or cilantro. Simmer for 10 minutes more. Serve hot.

Serves 6.

Pomegranate syrup, also known as pomegranate molasses, figures heavily in the flavoring of Middle Eastern soups. It is tart and tangy, a perfect foil for the heavy taste of lamb. It gives flavor to all manner of vegetable, bean, and meat soups. In a pinch, lemon is a substitute, but if you really want a true Middle Eastern flavor, buy a bottle in a specialty grocery store. It will keep well in the refrigerator. This red lentil and rice soup is enhanced by a generous addition of it.

Try to find the bright orange "red lentils." Along with the turmeric and pomegranate syrup, they will make the color of this soup beautiful.

Pomegranate Lentil Soup

         2 tablespoons butter
         1 onion, chopped
     1 1/2 quarts beef stock
       3/4 cup red lentils
       3/4 cup raw white rice
         1 teaspoon ground turmeric
         3 tablespoons pomegranate syrup
           salt and pepper to taste
       1/3 cup fresh cilantro, minced
         2 tablespoons fresh parsley, minced

Heat the butter in a soup pot and sauté the onion for 5 minutes. Pour in the stock and red lentils. Bring to a boil, reduce to a simmer, cover, and cook for 45 minutes, or until the lentils are almost tender.

Add the rice, turmeric, syrup, salt, and pepper. Continue to simmer for another 20 minutes.

Add the minced cilantro and let the soup rest for 10 minutes. Serve hot. Sprinkle each bowl with parsley.

Serves 6.

Whenever we travel, we ask hotel owners, merchants, guides, friends, and even people on the street where to go for the most authentic foods of the area. That is how we ended up in Petra, at a wonderful restaurant where the meal began with this soup.

But first let us tell you about one of the wonders of Jordan, the great rock city of Petra. It lies in a hidden valley about three hours south of Amman. We hired a guide and driver and set out early one morning. Once there, we had to travel, at first by horse, later on foot, through a narrow canyon called the Siq.

Finally, just when it seems the golden stone walls can get no closer, one emerges, and catches a first glance of the Treasury. The so-called Treasury is barely a building, more an elaborate two-tiered colonnaded facade carved from, and into, the surrounding rock. This magnificent structure is vaguely Roman in style, although carved by the Nabateans, who controlled the trade routes through the area over 2,000 years ago.

From this surprising beginning, we walked a mile or more into the valley proper. Once there, we realized that both high and low on the multi-colored canyon walls were dozens of equally stunning buildings. Most, like the Treasury, contained only small rooms. Their use is no longer clear—tombs, temples, meeting halls, theaters, storage areas. The Nabateans had their long-gone simple homes on the floor of the valley. Today, Bedouins live in the valley and help to run restaurants, hotels, and transportation.

The soup we ate that evening is a staple of the region. Ours was served with the meat separate from the rich wheat berry broth, accompanied by big sheets of flatbread. Wheat berries can be purchased at Middle Eastern food shops. They are whole, hulled wheat kernels and are also called *jareesh*.

Bedouin Lamb Stew

        2 tablespoons olive oil
        1 onion, chopped
        2 cloves garlic, minced
        2 pounds lamb meat and bones
          salt and pepper
    3/4 cup hulled, whole wheat berries
        3 cups beef stock
        1 tablespoon tomato paste
        1 2-inch cinnamon stick
    1/2 teaspoon cardamon seeds
        3 cups whole milk yogurt
        2 tablespoons cornstarch
    1/2 cup fresh parsley, minced
        1 lemon

In a soup pot, heat the oil and sauté the onion and garlic with the lamb pieces and bones. Add salt, pepper, and the wheat berries. Continue to sauté all for a few more minutes.

Pour in the stock. Put in the tomato paste, cinnamon, and cardamon. Bring to a boil, lower to a simmer, cover, and cook for 1 1/2 hours, or until the wheat berries and meat are tender. Remove the bones and cinnamon stick.

Mix the yogurt with the cornstarch and add it to the soup, stirring constantly, until it thickens.

Simmer for another 5 minutes. If you wish, take out the meat to serve separately. Or serve together in large flat bowls. Sprinkle with parsley, squeeze lemon on top.

Serves 4 to 6.

We tasted this unusual dish in northern Syria, near Aleppo. We understand that it is a favorite of the people in that region. Traditionally, it is eaten in the special way described in the recipe and served with flatbread.

One day in a restaurant in Amman, Jordan, we watched a woman make this incredible bread. She sat behind a very large inverted wok with a fire underneath. Taking a small ball of dough from a supply at her side, using just her hands, she rapidly shaped a paper-thin circle, fully two feet in diameter. She flipped it onto the convex pan, waited a minute, turned it over, and in another minute it was finished. It was folded into quarters and handed to a waiter. Each table got one or two for tearing into pieces to scoop food.

Lamb and Potato Soup

        2 tablespoons butter
        2 onions, finely chopped
        2 pounds lamb meat and bones
        2 quarts beef stock
          salt to taste
      1/4 teaspoon cayenne pepper
      1 1/2 cups yellow split peas
        2 large potatoes, peeled and cut into eighths
        1 teaspoon ground turmeric
          juice of 1 lemon
          flatbread

In a soup pot, heat the butter, then slowly sauté one of the onions, lamb pieces, and bones for 8 minutes.

Pour in the stock, salt, pepper, and peas. Bring to a boil, reduce to a simmer, cover, and cook about 1 hour, or until the peas are soft and the meat is tender.

Add the potatoes and turmeric and cook for another 15 minutes.

The traditional way to serve this soup is as follows: Scoop or strain out the potatoes, meat, and bones. Discard the bones. Chop and mash the meat, potatoes, remaining onion, and lemon juice to a paste.

Serve the pea broth first. Then the meat-potato mixture is scooped or spread onto Middle Eastern flatbread and served second.

Of course, this soup is great served as is. Just pick out the bones, and put in the remaining onion and lemon juice. Heat another few minutes to cook the last onion. Serve hot.

Serves 6 to 8.

St. Simon's Basilica, Syria

Hama is a charming city, really an overgrown village, located about half way between Damascus and Aleppo. We stayed there for several days, visiting the Roman city of Apamea and several of the Crusader castles in the area; and stumbled onto our own private chef! When the proprietor of our small hotel learned of our interest in history and local cuisines, he first arranged our transportation and then insisted that we take our meals at his place, because, he said, he had "the best cook of true Arabic (not tourist) food in the area." His cook turned out to be the local school teacher, who did cooking evenings. We were the only people staying there, and naturally requested that each meal have a different soup, but not lentil, as we had already sampled a half dozen varieties. Since he was cooking only for us, he was happy to oblige. I hope he is as good a teacher as he is a chef. We enjoyed several dishes each evening, including a green bean and lamb stew over burghul called *fasoolyeh,* and this delightful onion and cheese soup.

Hama Onion Cheese Soup

> 2 tablespoons *smen* (clarified butter), or butter
> 1 large onion, cut in a fine dice
> 1 quart chicken stock
> 1/4 teaspoon ground cinnamon (see note)
> 1/2 pound firm, mild, fresh, white cheese, such as rinsed
>   feta, Mexican white cheese, or Syrian cheese, diced

In a soup pot, heat the butter, and slowly cook the onion until soft. Add the stock and cinnamon, and simmer for 5 minutes. Add the finely diced cheese. Serve at once.

Serves 2.

Note: All over Syria we found pepper shakers containing ground cinnamon, cloves, or allspice in place of ground pepper. Since most foods, including their flatbread, contain traces of these spices, we thought this switch made lots of sense. Walking down a street in the Middle East at dinnertime, these are the aromas (rather than the olive oil and garlic of Spain and southern Italy) that one smells.

Temple, Egypt

North Africa—Soups of Egypt, Tunisia, and Morocco

The five Mediterranean countries stretching across the top of the African continent are, east to west, Egypt, Libya, Tunisia, Algeria, and Morocco. Their recorded history together stretches back 3,000 years, starting with the Phoenicians and the Romans, and 1,300 years ago, to the armies of Islam. Each occupier brought his preferred customs, culture, and cuisine. The Phoenicians and Romans introduced fig trees, olive cultivation for oil, and grapevines for wine. Around 700 A.D. the Muslim crusaders marched across North Africa, bringing with them the Arabic language, the Islamic religion, and spices, dates, citrus fruit, rice, almonds, butter, and sugar.

For 800 years, these Islamic conquerors of North Africa maintained a bastion of civilization, culture, and cuisine, while central Europe, to the north, remained ignorant and unsophisticated by comparison. Only Spain, Portugal, coastal France, and Sicily show any culinary influence of the Arabs.

The cuisine of North Africa was, and still is, masterfully flavored by tastes such as saffron, cinnamon, cumin, nutmeg, hot pepper, ginger, cardamon, cloves, rose water, preserved lemon, and turmeric. Like all of the Mediterranean, many of their savory dishes begin with olive oil, onion, tomatoes, and garlic; but from there, a sure and subtle hand takes over with those wonderful flavors and smells that define a dish from North Africa.

While the difference between the dishes of eastern Egypt and western Morocco are fairly marked, the regional changes are subtle; for example, the Egyptians preferring more cumin and allspice and Moroccan cooks using more cinnamon and nutmeg.

Overall, Morocco probably has the most sophisticated cuisine. As a region, it is isolated to the west, which has served to allow cooks there to develop dishes found nowhere else. Their most famous soup is *harira*, which uses butter to cook lamb, vegetables, and spices in a lemony sauce. An herb mixture called *tekliyah* is a marinade for finishing soups. Dried fruits are used in savory dishes.

Moving east to Tunisia and Algeria, one encounters *brik*, a deep-fried raw egg in pastry, and the fiery-hot condiment *harissa*. Couscous is eaten all over North Africa. Finally in Egypt, so far east its cuisine is often included with that of the Middle East, the people eat *molokhia* soup daily (see pages 153 and 203).

To travel to the countries of North Africa is to have the same cultural shocks as are experienced in travel to the Middle East. No matter how small we think the world has become, there is something so different here that our western eyes and sensibilities need time to adjust. Most people arrive by air into Casablanca, Tunis, or Cairo. These are the big cities and many people here, men and women, have adopted western dress. It is only after one begins to travel to the smaller towns and rural areas that one begins to perceive the differences.

A generous hospitality takes over. Big smiles, open homes, intriguing marketplaces, engaging children, new sights, smells, and tastes—all this and more bombards the senses. One is struck by the awareness that here in North Africa, parallel but incredibly different lives from ours are being lived.

So, finish with us our clockwise journey around the Mediterranean. Just a few miles across the Strait of Gibraltar lie Portugal and Spain, where we began. In 711 A.D., a combined army of Berbers, who are the natives of North Africa, and Muslims from the East crossed over to conquer Spain. They brought all of their culture and foods with them. They would remain until 1492, when they were forced back to Morocco. Their culinary imprint, however, remains to this day.

Our first experience of North Africa came as we descended the gangway of a boat from Spain into Tangiers, Morocco. What a surprise it was! The first thing we noticed was that all of the people wore *djellabahs,* the long robes used for street wear.

After settling in a hotel, we walked to the central *souk* or market of the old city and found it packed with men and women buying food. It was the holy month of Ramadan, the ninth month of the Muslim calendar, when observant Muslims fast from sunrise to sunset. This accounted for the unusual level of late-day hustle and bustle, as each family sought to buy and prepare dinner by 8:30.

The variety of items for sale was quite amazing. Many we had never seen before. Some of the fruits, vegetables, nuts, seeds, beans, herbs, spices, and animal parts were strange to our eyes. We spent about an hour there before returning to our hotel.

That evening, at a typical Moroccan-style restaurant, we feasted on Ramadan's traditional fast-breaking soup of *harira,* followed by big steaming dishes of couscous. *Harira* is said to have Berber origins and is the most well-known soup of Morocco.

Harira

  2 tablespoons butter
  2 stalks celery with leaves, chopped
  2 onions, chopped
  1 pound lean lamb, cut into small cubes
  1 teaspoon turmeric
  1/2 teaspoon ground black pepper
  1 teaspoon cinnamon
  1 teaspoon freshly grated ginger
1 1/2 quarts beef stock
  1 14-ounce can diced tomatoes
  1 cup dry lentils
  1/2 cup fresh parsley, minced
  1/4 cup fresh cilantro, minced

juice 1 lemon (4 tablespoons)
2 eggs
salt to taste
additional cinnamon
additional lemon juice

In a soup pot, melt the butter and slowly sauté the celery, onions, and lamb for 8 minutes. Add the turmeric, pepper, cinnamon, ginger, stock, tomatoes, and lentils. Bring to a boil, reduce to a simmer, cover, and cook for 1^1/$_2$ hours, or until the lamb and lentils are tender.

Add the parsley and cilantro. Beat the lemon and eggs together. Stirring continuously, slowly add the egg mix to the soup.

Bring back to a simmer for 5 minutes more. Add salt to taste.

Serve hot, sprinkled with cinnamon, with extra lemon juice on the side.

Serves 6.

All along the coast of North Africa, in small towns and cities like Tangiers and Tunis, fish is plentiful, and fish soups are as popular as they are in southern France and Spain. It is the spices and condiments that set them apart.

We were in Tunis with friends, preparing to take a one-week trip south. Along with a Tunisian woman and a French couple, we hired a 4-wheel drive vehicle and driver to take us to Speitla, Tozeur, Matmata, Djerba, Sousse, and El Jem to see the fabled and romantic desert oases, Roman ruins, and exotic landscapes we had read about.

Earlier we had visited the museum of ancient Carthage, both Phoenician and Roman, to see 2,000-year-old sculpture and mosaics. Later we wandered through the old quarter or *medina.*

Finally, we all met for dinner at a very beautiful and typically Tunisian restaurant. Walls and ceilings were ablaze with tiny mirrored mosaics and the seats, bolsters, and cushions were upholstered in a myriad of patterns. Large, highly polished brass trays sat on low stands, ready to receive drinks and appetizers. There was the sound of tinkling fountains and low music. The scent of jasmine and incense filled the air.

The meal was elaborate and began with small bowls of a light fish soup.

Moroccan Fish Soup

    1/2 onion, minced
    1 clove garlic, minced
    2 tablespoons olive oil
    1 quart chicken stock
    1 tablespoon tomato paste
    1 teaspoon cumin
    1/4 cup fresh cilantro, minced
    1/2 pound firm, white, fish fillets, cut into small cubes
    1/2 tablespoon preserved lemon, minced (see page 250)
        juice of 1/2 lemon

salt to taste

1 recipe of tekliyah (page 244) *or* harissa (page 251)

In a soup pot, lightly sauté the onion and garlic in the oil. Pour in the stock, tomato paste, cumin, and cilantro. Bring to a boil, lower to a simmer, cover, and cook for 10 minutes.

Add the fish, preserved lemon, lemon juice, and salt. Simmer for 5 minutes or until the fish is opaque.

Serve hot with either sauce on the side.

Serves 4.

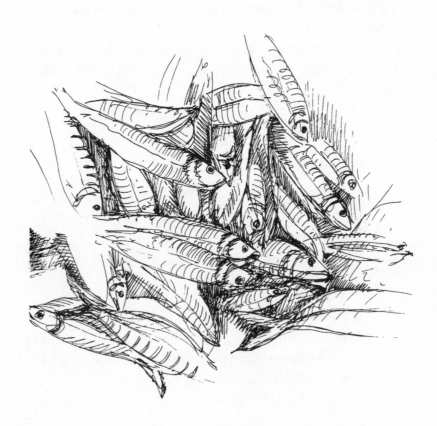

We ate this soup one evening at a hotel near the ancient Roman ruins in Speitla, Tunisia. It is strangely reminiscent of the Greek avgolemono soups, with their final egg-lemon addition. This one, though, was all North African, with its harissa and specialized spices.

In isolated areas, hotel food can be fairly awful. Their attempt to recreate what they believe to be European "haute cuisine" for a captive audience falls flat. But earlier in the day we had seen enough of the local restaurants, the most startling example of which was a cement block building with a real camel's head nailed to the door to advertise the meat special! We would take our chances with the hotel's fare! This soup turned out to be delicious.

Tunisian Avgolemono Soup

       2 tablespoons butter
       1 onion, chopped
     1/2 pound bone-in chicken, cut in pieces
       1 quart chicken stock
     1/4 teaspoon ground cinnamon
     1/4 teaspoon ground turmeric
     1/4 teaspoon ground cardamon *or* cardamon seeds
     1/4 teaspoon harissa, page 251, *or* 1/8 teaspoon cayenne
         pepper
     1/2 cup small pasta, such as orzo or stars
     1/3 cup fresh cilantro, minced
       2 eggs
         juice of 1 lemon

In a soup pot, melt the butter and sauté the onion and chicken pieces for several minutes. Pour in the stock. Add the cinnamon, turmeric, cardamon, and harissa or cayenne pepper. Bring to a boil, reduce to a simmer, cover, and cook for 45 minutes.

Take out the chicken and bones. Take all the chicken off the bones and chop. Return it to the soup and discard the bones.

Put the pasta and cilantro in the pot and cook for 10 minutes.

Beat the eggs and lemon juice together and slowly add to the soup, stirring constantly. Heat again, but do not let it boil. Serve hot.

Serves 4.

Market, Fez, Morocco

The second day after we arrived in Tangiers, we were talking to an English couple at our hotel, and we decided to drive south together to the market town of Tetuoan. We would leave the next morning.

The city rapidly fell away and soon we were in the desert, headed toward the Atlas Mountains. Small mud brick houses, walls, and farm buildings dot the landscape. An occasional camel and a few children leading a donkey along the road were the only signs of life.

After about an hour we were in Tetuoan. Although still some distance from the Berber homeland nearer the mountains, the market was crowded with these native desert people, both buying and selling. They were easily distinguished by their striped cotton shawls, which the women wear over their heads and around their shoulders and bodies in several layers.

The market here, as in Tangiers, is full of beautiful handicrafts and strange foods. Many live animals, mainly small birds, chickens, and rabbits destined for the stew pot, are for sale. We wandered, looked, and photographed for an hour, then sought out a restaurant for lunch. The soup we ate tasted somewhat like a liquid couscous, with a distinct anise flavor.

Couscous Soup

> 1 quart chicken stock
> 1 teaspoon aniseed *or* fennel seeds
> 1/4 cup fresh cilantro, minced
> 1/8 teaspoon saffron threads
> 1/2 cup couscous
> 3 tablespoons butter
> salt and pepper to taste

Put all ingredients in a soup pot. Bring to a boil, then reduce to a simmer. Cook for 5 minutes. Serve immediately or it will become too thick.

Serves 4.

Driving across the desert after lunch on a summer's day is pretty stupid. That, however, is just what we did between Tangiers and Fez. By a miracle, we arrived after 5 hours, hot, dry, and dusty. Lots of water, showers, and naps somewhat restored us.

The next day we went with a guide through the ancient and complex medina of old Fez. Dating from 800 A.D., it is entered through imposing gates and is a warren of winding streets and alleys with schools, mosques, shops, and homes. Small burros carry everything along passageways where no vehicle could go. Each street or section is devoted to a particular item or craft. There are the weaving, metalworking, and furniture-making areas, and whole streets where merchants sell spices, live animals, or vegetables.

The most compelling area is the tannery, where hides are cured and dyed in bubbling tubs. Men, dressed in the skimpiest of rags, walk catwalks to stir giant pots. The heat and smell are staggering, barely aided by the sprigs of mint that nearly everyone buys to hold under his nose. It is a sight we will never forget.

Hours later, as the intense heat of the day abated, we walked to what is basically the new city, built by the French in the early 1900s. There we started our dinner with a refreshing cold soup very reminiscent of Spanish gazpacho. Actually, the forerunner of white gazpacho (see page 31) was carried to Spain from Morocco by Muslims in 700 A.D.

Moroccan Gazpacho

      2 tablespoons olive oil
      1 large onion, chopped
      1 stalk celery, chopped
      2 carrots, peeled and chopped
      2 cloves garlic, chopped
   1/2 teaspoon cumin
   1/2 teaspoon ground turmeric
      1 quart chicken stock
      1 14-ounce can diced tomatoes
         juice of 1/2 lemon *or* 2 tablespoons vinegar
      2 teaspoons preserved lemon, page 250, minced
   1/2 cup fresh cilantro, minced
         salt and pepper to taste
   1/3 cup heavy cream (optional)

In a soup pot, heat the oil and sauté the onion, celery, carrots, and garlic. Add the cumin, turmeric, stock, and tomatoes.

Bring to a boil, reduce to a simmer, cover, and cook for 30 minutes.

Purée the soup in batches. Stir in the lemon juice or vinegar, preserved lemon, cilantro, salt, pepper, and if you wish, heavy cream.

Chill thoroughly. Serve cold.

Serves 6.

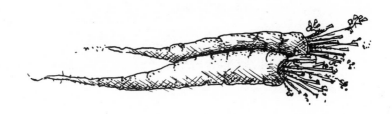

After a near-disastrous midday drive to Fez in the heat of the summer, we decided to return to Tangiers by a coastal road at first light. At 5:30 A.M. we were amazed to see the city fully awake and working. Farmers were tilling their fields in the half-light, getting in five hours of work before the real heat arrived.

We drove for three hours through mountains, arid hills, and flat lands, passing scenes that have not changed for thousands of years. The people live in mud brick houses, ride strong little donkeys, and draw their water from community wells.

Before reaching the coast to the west, we passed the Roman ruins of Lixus, standing alone in the desert. Here we stopped to eat some oranges, bread, and olives we had. Later, at a small town on the Atlantic, we found a restaurant for lunch. We had a chickpea stew.

There are dozens of variations on chickpea stew throughout North Africa. Its traditions go back thousands of years, when poor farmers had dried legumes, some fresh vegetables and herbs, and if they were lucky, a bit of meat to add to the stew pot. The spices were added by the Muslims after 700 A.D.

North African Chickpea Stew

    1 1/2 cups chickpeas, soaked overnight
    3 tablespoons butter
    1 tablespoon olive oil
    2 onions, chopped
    1 stalk celery, chopped
    1 tablespoon fresh ginger, peeled and minced
    1 teaspoon cumin
    1 teaspoon cinnamon
    1/2 teaspoon turmeric
    1 bay leaf
    1 pound meaty lamb bones
    1 pound chicken pieces
    2 quarts beef stock

    1 14-ounce can diced tomatoes
  1/2 teaspoon harissa, page 251, *or* 1/4 teaspoon cayenne
      pepper
  1/2 cup dry lentils
  1/2 cup small pasta shapes, such as orzo
  1/2 cup raisins
  1/2 cup fresh cilantro, minced *or* 1/2 cup fresh mint, minced
      salt to taste
      juice of 1 lemon
    1 tablespoon preserved lemon, page 250, minced
      additional cilantro *or* mint, minced
      additional harissa (optional)

Drain the chickpeas. Cover again with fresh water, bring to a boil, and cook for 1 hour. Drain and reserve.

In a soup pot, heat the butter and oil. Sauté the onions and celery for 5 minutes.

Add the ginger, cumin, cinnamon, turmeric, bay leaf, lamb, and chicken. Toss and mix over the heat to coat all with the spices and hot fat.

Pour in the stock. Add the reserved chickpeas, the tomatoes, harissa, and lentils.

Bring to a boil, reduce to a simmer, cover, and cook for 45 minutes. Remove the lamb and chicken. Pull all the meat off both. Discard the bones, chop the meat, and return it to the pot.

Add the pasta, raisins, cilantro or mint, salt, and lemon juice. Cook for another 15 minutes. Serve hot, sprinkled with preserved lemon, and cilantro or mint. Put the harissa in a small dish to pass.

Serves 6 to 8.

Another variation on North African chickpea stews, this one was given to us by Reina, who was born in Meknes, Morocco over 80 years ago.

Reina's Chickpea Soup

2 cups chickpeas, soaked in water overnight
2 tablespoons olive oil
1 onion, chopped
4 cloves garlic, chopped
1 carrot, peeled, and sliced thin
1 pound meaty lamb bones
1 14-ounce can diced tomatoes
1 teaspoon ground cumin
1 teaspoon fennel seeds
1/2 teaspoon turmeric
1 tablespoon fresh ginger, peeled and diced
1/2 teaspoon ground cinnamon

2 quarts beef stock
1/2 cup fresh cilantro, minced
1/4 cup green olives, pitted and chopped
1 tablespoon grated orange rind
salt and pepper to taste

Drain the chickpeas. Cover again with fresh water. Bring to a boil, reduce to a simmer, cover, and cook for 1 hour. Drain and reserve.

In a soup pot, heat the oil and sauté the onion, garlic, carrots, and meat bones.

Pour in the tomatoes. Add the cumin, fennel, turmeric, ginger, cinnamon, and stock.

Bring to a boil, lower to a simmer, add the drained chickpeas, and cook, covered, for another hour, or until the meat and chickpeas are very tender.

Remove the meat and bones. Pick any remaining meat off the bones and chop. Discard the bones. Return the meat to the soup. Add the cilantro, olives, orange rind, salt, and pepper. Simmer for 10 minutes. Serve hot.

Serves 6 to 8.

For us, one of the most interesting places we visited in Tunisia was an oasis near Tozeur. Wherever there is a spring or a river, people settle and build a small village.

In the distance, one sees a large patch of green surrounded by the endless sand. Upon arrival, one sees that it is long rows of stately date palms, covering many acres. Vegetables are planted below and around them. This two-tier system allows for the same water to serve all and for the trees to shade crops which could not grow out in the intense sun. Mud brick homes crowd the edges, trying to find some shade. Goats and sheep are tethered or penned nearby, also in the necessary shade of the date palms. Nothing is wasted—not space, and certainly not water.

In this particular oasis we stopped at a lively market, and bought sugar-sweet dates and a few pieces of the distinctive dark green and yellow Tunisian pottery. A restaurant nearby, really more of a stand, was serving hot bowls of this puréed Tunisian soup, accompanied by the fiery harissa. Use harissa with caution; it can be a bit tough on American stomachs. Tunisians love it and it comes with everything—sort of like catsup in a diner in the United States.

Oasis Chickpea Soup

    1$\frac{1}{2}$ cups dried chickpeas, soaked in water overnight
    1 onion, chopped
    6 cloves garlic, chopped
    1 carrot, peeled and cut in pieces
    1 stalk celery with leaves, chopped
    2 tablespoons olive oil
    2 quarts beef stock
    $\frac{1}{2}$ teaspoon hot red pepper flakes
    1 teaspoon cardamon seeds (out of the pods)
    1 teaspoon ground cumin
    $\frac{1}{2}$ cup fresh cilantro, minced
    1 cup yogurt
      salt to taste
    1 recipe harissa, page 251

Drain the soaked chickpeas. Cover again with fresh water. Bring to a boil, and simmer for 1 hour. Drain and reserve.

In a soup pot, sauté the onion, garlic, carrot, and celery in the oil.

Add the stock, drained chickpeas, hot pepper, cardamon, and cumin. Bring to a boil, reduce to a simmer, cover, and cook until the chickpeas are very tender.

When the soup has cooled a bit, purée in batches.

Return to the pot, stir in the cilantro, yogurt, and salt. Bring back to a simmer and cook for 5 minutes.

Serve hot with harissa on the side.

Serves 6 to 8.

Even today, in rural areas of North Africa, meat is still preserved by age-old methods. In the desert, the slaughter of a lamb for a special occasion means that rapid preservation is required to save the uneaten portions for another time. Women cut the excess meat into narrow strips and rub them with salt and spices. These are hung on long poles or strings and left to dry in the hot, arid air. They are either packed in fat or allowed to dehydrate. Later, a few pieces in a soup pot add body and nourishment to a winter meal.

Try to find *pastirma* in a Middle Eastern or Greek grocer or buy high-quality beef jerky in a health food store or grocer. This dish is a spicy stew, meant to be served over rice or couscous.

City gate,
Morocco

Preserved Meat Stew

>   2 tablespoons olive oil
>   1 onion, chopped
>   2 cloves garlic, chopped
>   1 quart beef stock
>   4 ounces beef jerky or pastirma, shredded
>   1/2 teaspoon cumin
>   1 teaspoon paprika
>   1/4 cup tomato paste
>   1/2 teaspoon harissa, page 251, *or* 1/4 teaspoon cayenne
>   pepper
>   1 cup dry white rice *or* couscous, prepared for serving
>   1/4 cup fresh mint, minced
>   salt to taste

In a soup pot, heat the oil and sauté the onion and garlic for 3 minutes.

Pour in the stock, jerky or pastirma, cumin, paprika, tomato paste, and harissa or pepper.

Bring to a boil, lower to a simmer, cover, and cook for 1 hour, or as long as it takes to make the meat tender.

In the meantime, prepare the rice or couscous according to package instructions.

When the meat is tender, add the mint and salt to taste. Serve over bowls of rice or couscous. Pass additional harissa.

Serves 4.

Dried fruits are often incorporated into the savory dishes of North Africa. Raisins (from those original Roman grapevines), dried apricots, and figs find their way into the soups and stews, especially in Morocco. Here is a classic combination of lamb and apricots, teamed with the herbs and spices that make it taste like North African cuisine.

Moroccan Lamb and Apricot Stew

    2 pounds lean lamb pieces and bones
    3 tablespoons olive oil
    5 cloves garlic, chopped
    1 onion, chopped
    3 cups beef stock
    3 cups chicken stock
    1 teaspoon ground turmeric
    1 tablespoon fresh ginger, peeled and minced
  1/4 teaspoon saffron
    1 teaspoon ground cinnamon
    1 14-ounce can diced tomatoes
    1 cup dried apricots, chopped
  1/2 cup slivered almonds
  1/4 cup fresh mint, minced
     juice of 1 lemon
     salt and pepper to taste
     prepared couscous, enough for 6

In a soup pot, brown the lamb pieces in the oil. After 5 minutes, add the garlic and onions. Continue to sauté for 3 more minutes. Do not let the garlic brown.

Pour in the two stocks, bring to a boil, lower to a simmer, cover, and cook for 45 minutes, or until the lamb is nearly tender.

Remove the lamb and bones from the soup. Discard the bones after pulling off any meat. Cut the meat into a large dice and return it to the pot.

Add the turmeric, ginger, saffron, cinnamon, tomatoes, and apricots. Cover and simmer for 30 minutes.

Add the almonds, mint, lemon, salt, and pepper. Cook for 10 more minutes. Serve over prepared couscous.

Serves 6.

Vegetable soups are ubiquitous. All over the world, cooks take the fresh produce and herbs of the area and combine them to make nourishing meals for their families. What are different, of course, are the special ingredients that stamp each with the character of that country's cuisine.

Smen is clarified butter from North Africa, similar to *ghee* in India. Once all the liquid and impurities have been cooked out of it, pure butter will store for long periods of time without spoiling.

Couscous is precooked, cracked semolina. It is widely available in the specialty food section of supermarkets. Smen, couscous, preserved fruits, cinnamon, turmeric, ginger, and cilantro make this vegetable soup typical of North Africa.

North African Vegetable Soup

      2 tablespoons butter *or* smen
      1 onion, chopped
      1 carrot, peeled and sliced thin
      1 medium zucchini, cubed
    1/2 pound green beans, cut in 1-inch lengths
      1 large potato, peeled and cubed
      1 14-ounce can diced tomatoes

    1 cup *(total)* prunes, raisins, dried figs, and/or dried
        apricots, diced
    1 tablespoon preserved lemon, page 250, minced,
  1/8 teaspoon harissa, page 251, *or* cayenne pepper
  1/2 teaspoon ground cinnamon
  1/2 teaspoon turmeric
  1/2 teaspoon cumin
    1 teaspoon grated fresh ginger
1 1/2 quarts chicken stock
  1/2 cup fresh cilantro, minced
        salt to taste
        juice of 1/2 lemon
    1 cup couscous, prepared according to package
        instructions

In a soup pot, heat the butter and sauté the onion and carrot for 5 minutes. Add all the vegetables, dried fruits, preserved lemon, spices, and stock.

Bring to a boil, reduce to a simmer, cover, and cook for 30 minutes.

Add the cilantro, salt, and lemon juice. Cook for 10 more minutes. Serve hot over prepared couscous.

Serves 6.

This soup is made with generous amounts of chicken, tomatoes, mint, and, once again, typical North African spices.

North African Chicken Tomato Soup

    2 tablespoons butter
    1 onion, chopped
 1½ pounds skinless chicken pieces with bones
    2 14-ounce cans diced tomatoes
    1 quart chicken stock
  ½ teaspoon cumin
  ½ teaspoon turmeric
  ½ teaspoon cinnamon
  ⅛ teaspoon harissa, page 251, or cayenne pepper
      salt to taste
  ½ cup fresh mint, minced
    1 tablespoon lemon juice
    1 cup couscous, prepared according to package
      instructions

In a soup pot, melt the butter, and sauté the onion and chicken pieces for 5 minutes.

Pour in the tomatoes and stock. Add the cumin, turmeric, cinnamon, harissa, and salt.

Bring to a boil, reduce to a simmer, cover, and cook for 45 minutes, or until the chicken is tender.

Take the chicken out, remove the bones, chop the meat, and add back to the soup. Discard the bones.

Add the mint and lemon juice. Simmer for 10 minutes. Serve hot over prepared couscous.

Serves 4.

The French controlled most of North Africa until the mid-20th century. Parts of the urban architecture is typically French, as are the baguettes and croissants that you can still buy in Tunis and Tangiers. Even with a bit of bad French, one can get along.

We ate this soup in a French restaurant in Tangiers, Morocco. It is a perfect marriage of continental-style cooking with Moroccan scents and flavors.

Moroccan-Style Cream of Carrot Soup

1 quart chicken stock
4 carrots, peeled and sliced
1 small onion, chopped
1 small potato, peeled and diced
1 tablespoon tomato paste
1/8 teaspoon cinnamon
1/4 teaspoon cumin
1/4 teaspoon turmeric
a pinch cayenne pepper
juice of 1/2 lemon
salt to taste
1 tablespoon grated orange rind
1/2 cup heavy cream
1/4 cup fresh parsley, minced

In a soup pot, put all the ingredients except the cream and parsley.

Bring to a boil, reduce to a simmer, cover, and cook for 30 minutes.

When the soup has cooled a bit, purée it in batches.

Return it to the pot and add the cream. Bring it to a simmer again.

Serve hot, or chill thoroughly overnight and serve cold. Sprinkle each serving with parsley.

Serves 4.

The best and easiest way to see the Egyptian temples at Luxor, the sights at Memphis, Karnak, Philae, Kom Ombo, and Edfu, and the Valley of the Kings and Queens, is to take a boat down the Nile River. It becomes a floating hotel for five or six wonderful days on the placid river, where one can see the people of the countryside going about their daily lives. They are mostly farmers, cultivating the narrow, irrigated ribbon of fertile green land bordering the water. Each day the boat stops and visits are paid to different ancient sites.

We took this boat trip, then returned to spend a few more days in the bustling city of Cairo. There, we visited the famous Khalili *souk,* or market, bought some small gifts for friends and family, and ate in a recommended restaurant in the old city. We knew that the most popular soup in Egypt is *molokhia* soup. Its origin is said to go back 4,000 years and was eaten daily by humble people then, as it is now. We wanted to try a bowl. It was not hard to find and the restaurant owner seemed very pleased that we wished to sample this "non-tourist" dish. It turned out to be somewhat similar to the Molokhia Soup (page 153) that we ate in Jordan. It uses the same vegetable. Buy frozen molokhia in a Middle Eastern grocer.

Egyptian Chicken Molokhia Soup

    1 1/2 quarts chicken stock
    1 1/2 pounds bone-in chicken, cut into 5 or 6 pieces
    1 14-ounce can diced tomatoes
    1 onion, chopped
    1/2 pound frozen molokhia (mlookhiyah)
       juice of 1 lemon
       salt and pepper to taste
       a large pot of cooked, hot, white rice
    1 recipe tekliyah sauce, page 244

In a soup pot, combine the stock, chicken, tomatoes, and onion. Bring to a boil, reduce to a simmer, cover, and cook for 1 hour, or until the chicken is tender.

Remove the chicken and bones from the soup, and strip off the meat. Discard the bones. Chop the meat into small pieces.

Return the meat to the pot, along with the thawed molokhia, lemon juice, salt, and pepper. Return to a simmer, and cook, uncovered, for 10 minutes.

In the meantime, prepare the sauce as instructed. Set aside.

Serve the soup, hot, spooned over bowls of rice. Each diner adds a little of the sauce on top.

Serves 6.

Bonifacio, Corsica

The Soups of
the Mediterranean Islands

. . . .

There are six or seven major islands in the Mediterranean, and thousands of smaller ones. By and large, their cuisines are typical of the Mediterranean, full of those ingredients with which we have become so familiar. They often prepare foods in the same way as those parts of the mainland to which they lie closest. But this is not always true. The word *isola,* meaning "island" in Italian, has lent us the word *isolated.* This concept of isolation makes the cuisines of certain islands in the Mediterranean unique, and eccentric enough to deserve the attention of a separate chapter.

Most of the islands, like Sicily, Sardinia, Malta, Cyprus, and the smaller Greek islands have several things in common that are unique to them. First, they are poor and somewhat arid. Historically, life was hard and farming was precarious. The people made do with wild animals like boar, small birds, rabbits, and seafood, and gathered foods such as fennel, field herbs and greens, mushrooms, capers, prickly pears, and chestnuts.

In addition, all have had to play host to virtually every conquering culture, lying as they do as natural stepping stones and strategic defense points. This layering of history can still easily be seen in the features of the people, as well as in their architecture, languages, and foods.

And last, by definition, all islands have a shared heritage of the sea. It has provided their sustenance, and paradoxically, kept them isolated while carrying their invaders to them.

. . . .

There is a magic about going to any island, big or small, and a melancholy when it is time to leave. The omnipresent rhythm of the waves, the smell of the salt air, the cooling breezes, entering through a port where life has been going on before your arrival; all is exciting—the beginning of a new adventure. Arrival by boat, especially, contributes to the feeling that life, even for a while, can be fully enclosed and understood.

Cefalu, Sicily

Sicily

Lying just three miles off Italy's "toe," Sicily is an ancient land with an exotic past. The Greeks, Romans, Arabs, Normans, and Spanish have built settlements, and each in turn, to a greater or lesser degree, has ruled this biggest of the Mediterranean islands. Sicily's strategic position has made it one of history's most prized pieces of real estate, while at the same time, its great size has set it apart as its own kingdom.

Today, only ninety miles from North Africa, it is a melting pot, and stubbornly retains traces of its Arab past. While it is officially part of Italy, its cuisine is unique. It is the home of *caponata* (a cooked eggplant antipasto), *pasta con le sarde* (sardine and anchovy sauce for pasta), and sweets such as *cassata, marzipan, cannoli, zabaglione,* and *granita*.

Savory dishes are often sharpened with the addition of home-grown, hot, red peppers, rather than black peppercorns, because, it is said, their historic poverty did not allow them the much more expensive spice.

All of Sicily is an arid and harsh landscape, but the middle of this enormous island is austerely beautiful. Covered with olive trees, dirt roads lined with prickly pear hedgerows, and the old stone buildings of long-ago abandoned farms, there is only the buzz of cicadas to keep one company.

We were driving through central Sicily, to Piazza Armerina, to tour the exceptional 4th-century Roman hunting lodge there. Our guidebooks said that the mosaics were especially fine, and they were. All over the Roman world artisans created elaborate tile floors in the homes of the rich. They have remained bright and beautiful to this day, and provide a pictorial insight into their lives. The floors of this villa were covered with millions of tiny tiles, depicting hunting scenes, sporting events, and pictures from everyday life. It is thought to be one of the homes of an emperor, covering over 12,000 square feet.

At the other end of the spectrum were the poor. For thousands of years, they eked out a living by relying on wild plants and animals for their sustenance. Inland peasants never tasted seafood, but if they were lucky, they had a bit of game to go with the wild fennel that grows everywhere. The combination of pork and fennel is still a popular one. Most Italian sausage uses a combination of garlic and fennel for seasoning.

In the main town, a few miles away from the villa, we ate in a family-style restaurant, where we chose a ground pork and fennel soup as a first course. We could imagine that such a soup was eaten, if not by the peasants, then certainly in the hunting villa. Woe to the poor farmer who poached the emperor's wild boar!

Sicilian Fennel and Pork Soup

    1 tablespoon olive oil
    1/2 pound fresh Italian-style pork sausage
    1 onion, chopped
    2 cloves garlic, minced
    1/4 teaspoon fennel seed
    1 head fennel (stalks removed), sliced thin
    1 quart chicken stock
    1/2 cup small pasta shapes, such as orzo
        salt and pepper to taste
    1/2 cup freshly grated pecorino cheese

In a soup pot, heat the oil. Remove the sausage from its casing, break it up, and sauté in the oil for 5 minutes.

Add the onion and garlic and continue to sauté for another 5 minutes.

Add the fennel seeds, fennel, and stock. Bring to a boil, reduce to a simmer, and cook for 35 minutes.

Add in the pasta, salt, and pepper. Simmer, uncovered, for 10 minutes. Serve hot, with cheese on top of each serving.

Serves 4.

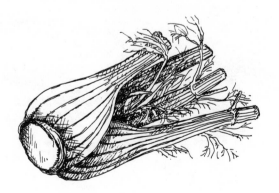

Erice is perched on a high cliff overlooking the Mediterranean, at the extreme western point of Sicily. It has been there since the Greeks settled it, over 2,000 years ago. Today, however, when one walks the narrow cobblestone streets, one is reminded of a later age, when the Arabs, then the Normans, occupied the site.

Down below in Trapani, where the ferries leave for Tunisia, men fish for tuna. There, and throughout Sicily, tuna figures heavily in their fish dishes. In Trapani and Erice, several restaurants serve a Sicilian version of North African couscous, made with fish rather than chicken.

Sicilian Fish Couscous

2 tablespoons olive oil
1 clove garlic, minced
1 onion, quartered
1 carrot, peeled and sliced
1 14-ounce can diced tomatoes
1 turnip, peeled and sliced
1 zucchini, sliced
1 quart chicken stock
1 pound tuna fillets, cut in 1-inch cubes

1/4 teaspoon saffron

1/2 teaspoon ground cinnamon

1/4 to 1/2 teaspoon hot red pepper flakes

1/2 cup raisins

1/2 cup fresh parsley, minced

1/4 cup fresh cilantro, minced

salt and pepper to taste

2 cups couscous, prepared according to package instructions

2 lemons

In a soup pot, heat the oil and sauté the garlic, onion, and carrot for 4 minutes.

Pour in the tomatoes, then add the turnip, zucchini, and stock. Bring to a boil, reduce to a simmer, cover, and cook for 30 minutes.

Add the tuna pieces, saffron, cinnamon, red pepper, raisins, parsley, cilantro, salt, and pepper. Simmer for 5 minutes, or until the tuna is cooked through.

Put generous mounds of couscous in each of 4 wide soup bowls. Divide and spoon the soup over top. Squeeze a bit of 1 lemon over each bowl. Cut the other lemon into quarters and place a piece on each serving.

Serves 4.

Palermo, Sicily's capital, is one of the most chaotic cities in Europe. Automobile traffic appears to follow no rules, its famous architecture is falling into ruin, bits of paper and plastic water bottles accumulate in the streets, vendors shout for attention . . . it's all very confusing.

We had been sightseeing for several days, both in the city and outside, at Monreale, the great 12th-century Norman church. Late in the day we visited the bustling Vucciria, a souk-like marketplace in old Palermo. Even by Palermo's standards, this market is loud. Vendors delivered an unceasing chant at the top of their voices, selling their olives, vegetables, meat, and fish. All side streets led to the main market square where five or six fires were going. Trash was burning and street vendors were cooking.

We found the sign for a second floor restaurant and were shown to a table on a minuscule terrace overlooking it all. It felt like the opening scene of a great Italian opera, with us in balcony box seats! As we sat sipping wine and eating a dinner of soup and delicious stuffed calamari, we found Palermo, for all its noise and chaos, a most fascinating and exotic city.

The light soup we ate seemed a variation on the mainland *stracciatella* (page 83). The taste was the same, but the strands were made into small dumplings.

Sicilian Egg Dumpling Soup

    1¹/2 quarts chicken stock
      4 eggs
    1¹/2 cups fresh breadcrumbs (not packaged)
      2 cups grated pecorino cheese
      1 large garlic clove, crushed and minced
        salt and pepper to taste
    ¹/4 cup fresh parsley, minced

In a soup pot, bring the stock to a simmer.

Beat the eggs very well. Add the breadcrumbs, cheese, garlic, salt, pepper, and parsley.

Mix and beat the above together thoroughly. You should have a light batter or loose dough, that can be pushed off a teaspoon into the simmering stock. Add a bit more bread and cheese if it does not hold together well.

Using two teaspoons, scoop up some batter with one and push it off into the stock with the other. Work quickly, so that all the dumplings go into the stock within several minutes.

Continue to simmer until they float to the top, and then 2 minutes more.

Season the soup with additional salt and pepper if necessary. Serve hot.

Serves 4 to 6.

Sardinia

Sardinia, part of Italy, is a big, rugged, scenic island, and except for the northeastern Costa Smeralda, playground of the rich, is seldom visited. It holds its secrets fast in the nearly inaccessible inland mountains, home to strange prehistoric structures. Its residents are hospitable but wary; historically, invaders have driven them to the relative safety of their mountains.

Except along the coasts, where the people have always enjoyed seafood, the cuisine of Sardinia is centered around wild foods—game, mushrooms, field herbs, prickly pears, chestnuts, honey, sheep-milk cheese, grains and legumes, and those vegetables that grow well there, such as potatoes, tomatoes, garlic, onions, fennel, and cabbage. Their favorite method of cooking big pieces of meat is pit-roasting, and they do not eat nearly as much pasta as mainland Italians. Sardinian bread is often served in thin, crisp sheets called *carasau,* rather than in fat loaves. Their pecorino cheeses, both fresh and mature, are delicious.

History passes slowly in Sardinia, and many foods are reminiscent of past cultures. Bouillabaisse *(zimino),* couscous, paella, and herbs such as saffron, are all reminders of visits from the French, Spanish, and Arabs.

Favorite "gathered" foods in Sardinia are its wild mushrooms and thistles. In the thistle family, artichokes are cultivated in both Italy and Sardinia, where they are perennial favorites. The two vegetables combine beautifully in this earthy vegetable soup.

Sardinian Artichoke Mushroom Soup

> 4 ounces pancetta or bacon, diced
> 2 cloves garlic, minced
> 1½ pounds portobella and other varieties of domestic or
>   wild mushrooms, sliced thin or diced
> 2 tablespoons olive oil
> 2 14-ounce cans artichoke hearts (not marinated)
> 5 cups chicken stock
> ½ cup fresh parsley, minced
> 1 tablespoon fresh rosemary, minced
>   salt and pepper to taste

In a soup pot, lightly brown the pancetta or bacon. Add the garlic and mushrooms. Add up to 2 tablespoon of oil if necessary. Sauté all for 5 minutes.

Drain the artichokes and cut in eighths. Add them to the pot along with the stock, parsley, rosemary, salt, and pepper.

Bring to a boil, reduce to a simmer, and cook for 15 minutes. Serve hot.

Serves 4.

Sardinians save every scrap of bread, and eventually this dry bread finds its way into a simple soup casserole called *suppaquata* (water soup). Every village has its own, and we tasted several while we were there. I've tried to combine their common ingredients. This soup tastes like the ones we ate.

Suppaquata

1/4 pound pancetta or bacon, diced
  3 tablespoons olive oil
1/2 loaf stale country-style bread, cut thick
  4 cloves garlic, minced
1/2 cup fresh parsley, minced
1/4 cup fresh basil, minced
  1 teaspoon *each,* fresh minced rosemary, sage, and thyme
  6 ounces fresh pecorino *or* feta cheese, crumbled
  6 ounces grated jack *or* munster cheese
    salt and pepper to taste
3 to 4 cups chicken stock
1/2 cup freshly grated hard pecorino cheese

In a skillet, fry the pancetta or bacon until crisp. Removed from the pan, but leave the fat. Add enough olive oil to fry the bread on each side. You may have to parcel out the oil so that the first bread slices don't absorb it all.

In the remaining oil, lightly sauté the garlic, then put all the herbs and reserved pancetta into the pan.

Divide the bread and the two soft cheeses in half. In a deep casserole, place a layer of bread, half of the cheese, and half of the garlic-herb mix. Then make a second sequence of bread, cheese, and garlic-herb mix.

Add salt and pepper to the stock if needed. Remember, the cheese and bacon are salty. Pour the stock carefully over the top of the casserole layers. Allow it to soak in. Add more if needed. It should be quite wet.

Sprinkle the top with the grated pecorino cheese.

Bake in a preheated 350° oven for 45 minutes, or until bubbling. Remove from the oven and allow it to set for 15 minutes. Serve in wide flat soup bowls.

Serves 4.

Generally speaking, there are simply no tourists in the inland of Sardinia. Although all of Europe visits its Costa Smeralda, a posh resort area on the northeast coast, very little can induce visitors to drive inland for hours, over winding mountain roads to an area with few services. One definite attraction, though, is the remains of Bronze Age settlements scattered over hundreds of sites. Unique to Sardinia, they are basalt dry-stone constructions called *nuraghi,* which always include a fortress tower, surrounded by the circular stone huts of the people. Archaeologists have unearthed thousands of bronze weapons and small bronze sculptures of people and animals. Most of these are housed in a beautiful new museum in Cagliari.

Just driving along, it is possible to observe nuraghi in the distant fields and hills, but we also made a special trip inland to what is considered the best site. With a guide, small groups are allowed to climb up in the tower (now only half its height) and walk through what remains of individual homes. We were lucky to find an English-speaking guide. Illustrated signs are in English, Sardinian, and Italian. The stone moving, fitting, and building skills of these people, 4,000 years ago, is truly amazing.

There is a town nearby where we stopped for lunch, which we quickly learned is the main meal of the day. The appetite of the Sardinians is astonishing. We witnessed multiple courses being served and consumed; in contrast, we ate only soup accompanied by one or two antipasti. This day we had another soup in the mountain tradition of Sardinia. Once again it uses gathered, as well as cultivated, vegetables, and a bit of pecorino cheese.

Sardinian Mountain Soup

> 2 tablespoons olive oil
> 3 cloves garlic, minced
> 6 cups mixed greens, such as sorrel, dandelion, chicory, escarole, mustard, and arugula
> 2 potatoes, peeled and diced
> 1 quart chicken stock
>   salt and pepper to taste
> 1/2 cup freshly grated pecorino cheese

In a soup pot, heat the oil and sauté the garlic for 2 minutes. Add the washed and coarsely chopped greens. Toss in the garlic oil to wilt them.

Add the potatoes, stock, salt, and pepper.

Bring to a boil, lower to a simmer, cover and cook for 20 minutes, or until the ingredients are tender.

Allow the soup to sit for 10 minutes, then serve. Sprinkle each serving with cheese.

Serves 4.

Alghero, Sardinia

Both main cities of Sardinia, Cagliari, its capital in the south, and Alghero in the north, are made for exploring. Both are ports, both are heavily Spanish in flavor and dialect, and both retain parts of old, walled cities of narrow streets and interesting architecture.

Cagliari's history goes back to Carthaginian times, but the castle that anchors the old city dates from the 1300s. We walked the restored cobblestone streets surrounding it on its high bluff, visited its archaeological museum, ducked into a local bar to wait out a sudden thunderstorm, and then enjoyed a spectacular sunset from the castle wall.

A week later we were in Alghero in the north, a much quieter seaport. Its old town is on flat harbor land. Once again, we spent some hours enjoying the streets, shops, and cathedral. It is said that the people here speak a dialect of Catalan, a remnant of their 14th-century Spanish occupation, but our linguistically-challenged ears could not detect it. Here in Alghero, our lunch in a small restaurant in the old quarter began with this extremely simple peasant soup. It is typical of Sardinian fare in its use of a handful of whole grains and a bunch of wild herbs.

Minty Grain Soup

> 3 cups chicken stock
> 3 cups beef stock
> 1 cup barley
> 3 ounces medium-hard pecorino cheese, cut in a 1/3-inch dice
> 1/8 teaspoon hot red pepper flakes
> salt to taste
> 1/4 cup fresh mint, minced

Heat the stocks in a pot and stir in the barley. Bring to a boil, reduce to a simmer, cover, and cook for 40 minutes, or until the barley is tender.

Add the cheese, pepper, salt, and mint. Simmer, stirring, until the cheese partially melts. Serve immediately.

Serves 4 to 6.

Corsica

· ·

A beautiful, wild, mountainous island, more Italian than French, it
is the birthplace of Napoleon and home to unspoiled scenery—chestnut forests, uncrowded beaches, and ancient ports. Its air is heavy
with the perfume of lavender, heather, and myrtle. It has its own language, which is closer to an Italian dialect than to French, and is said
to have had a history of fifty different invasions over the millennia.

For thousands of years, farmers and fishermen have relied on the
gifts of the land and sea for food. Corsica has a higher rainfall than
most southern parts of the Mediterranean and is big enough to support livestock, mostly sheep, goats, and pigs. Its pine and chestnut
forests abound with wild boars, rabbits, small birds, and honey, herbs,
and mushrooms.

The cuisine of Corsica relies on chestnuts and their flour to make
cakes, breads, cookies, fried cakes, and even beer. From their sheep and
goats come some of the best European cheeses, such as a soft ricotta-
like cheese called *brocciu*. From their pigs and wild boar come the
sought-after cured hams *(prisuttu)* and the many other pork products that form a big part of the Corsican diet.

We first tasted the glorious Corsican ham at a party the day after
Jacques and Thérèse Cornetti's daughter Christine got married. This
Corsican-French family hosted a luncheon at their country farmhouse
in Véséou, north of Nice. Relatives from Corsica brought whole,
cured hams covered in gray ash. Thin slices were carved and served,
along with wine, cheese, salad, fruit, and wonderful bread.

All those leftover ham bones eventually find their way into a traditional soup, called country or mountain soup. It is a slow-cooked
mix of herbs, vegetables, beans, and the smoky, salty goodness of the

· ·

ham bone, simmered for hours. I ate this soup in Corte, in the heart of old Corsica. It was served with crispy, chestnut-flour fritters and Corsican *brocciu* (ricotta) cheese.

Soupe de Montagne

> 1 meaty cured ham bone
> 1 cup assorted dried beans; a mix of white beans, lima beans, kidney beans, etc., soaked overnight
> 1½ quarts chicken stock
> 1 large potato, peeled and cubed
> 1 cup fresh string beans, cut in 1-inch lengths
> 1 onion, diced
> 1 sprig fresh thyme
> 1 tablespoon fresh rosemary leaves
> salt and pepper to taste

Put the ham bone in a soup pot. Drain the beans. Put them in the pot. Add the stock, cover, and simmer for 1 hour, or until the beans are nearly tender.

Add the potato, string beans, onion, thyme, rosemary, salt, and pepper. Cover and simmer for another 45 minutes, or until all is tender. This soup should be thick, but add water if it is too thick.

Remove the ham bone, cut off the meat, chop, and return to the soup. Discard the bone.

My soup was served with small plain croutons, which is an option, but not really necessary.

Serves 4.

On several occasions when we were in Corsica we had a meat stew called a *civit*. It can be made with rabbit, wild boar, or beef, and is rich with the taste of smoked bacon, wild mushrooms, and field herbs.

Corsican Meat Stew

      4 ounces thick-cut bacon, diced
      2 pounds lean beef, rabbit, *and/or* wild boar, cut in 1-inch
         cubes
      4 tablespoons flour
      2 onions, chopped
      1 pound assorted fresh mushrooms, such as porcini or
         portobella, washed, dried, and sliced
      1 cup dry red wine
    1/8 teaspoon cinnamon
      1 tablespoon fresh rosemary, chopped
      1 bay leaf
    1/2 tablespoon fresh thyme or sage, chopped
         salt and pepper to taste
      3 cups beef stock
      1 pound pasta, such as ziti

In a wide, covered, soup pot, slowly cook the bacon until it is crisp, and has given up its fat.

Dredge the meat in the flour and shake off the excess. Brown it in the bacon fat. Add 1 or 2 tablespoons of olive oil if there is not enough fat.

Add the onions, and continue to sauté the bacon, meat, and onions. Finally, add in the mushrooms. Cook over high heat for 5 minutes, turning frequently.

After the mushrooms start to cook, pour in the red wine. Allow it to boil and reduce for several minutes, then add the spices, herbs, salt, pepper, and stock.

Bring to a boil, reduce to a simmer, cover, and slow cook for 1 or 2 hours, or until the meat is very tender.

Cook the pasta according to package instructions. Drain it, and toss with the soup gravy. Serve the meat separately.

Serves 4.

Thérèse Cornetti, a friend who lives near Nice, France, gave us this recipe. It came from her grandmother, who was from Porto Vecchio, Corsica. She would prepare this as a fasting soup on the Thursday and Friday (Good Friday) before the feast of Easter. In old Corsica it was called . . .

"Soup of the Lord"

> 2 tablespoons olive oil
> 1 onion, chopped
> 1 tomato, peeled, seeded, and chopped
> 2 quarts water
> 1 pound dried red beans, soaked overnight
>   salt and pepper to taste
> 1/2 pound pasta, elbows or ziti

In a soup pot, heat the oil, and sauté the onion for 5 minutes. Add the tomato and water. Bring to a boil and lower to a simmer.

Drain the beans and add them to the soup pot, along with the salt and pepper. Cover and cook for 45 minutes, or until the beans are almost tender.

Add the pasta and cook for 15 minutes. Serve hot.

Serves 6.

Corsica, smaller than Sardinia, can be at least partially explored in a few days. We took the ferry from Sardinia, and over the next several days drove around the rugged Cap Corse in the north, with its dozens of medieval watchtowers built by the Genoans. We continued down through the center of the island to Corte, and finally to Bonifacio in the south.

The crisp fall days brought out the hunters and their dogs. More than once, we saw early morning parties out for wild boar, following the age-old traditions of the island. Then one morning, stopping along the road for coffee, we met a man who proudly showed us the two boars he had just shot. They would be eaten fresh, smoked, or made into the many varieties of sausages for sale everywhere.

That day we continued on to historic Corte, the center of the island and its resistance to foreign rule. It is high in the central mountains, its citadel overlooking all. The old town huddles at its feet. There is a museum of Corsican life there, a palace and a belvedere, as well as several excellent restaurants. In the same place where we enjoyed the Soupe de Montagne, page 223, we ate a wild boar stew with myrtle. Myrtle is a shrubby tree that grows wild everywhere in Corsica. It produces small red berries, which are made into liqueurs, sherbets, and jellies. Some myrtle liqueur is added to this stew.

Wild Boar Stew with Myrtle

 5 tablespoons olive oil
 1 cloves garlic, minced
 1 onion, sliced
 1 carrot, peeled and sliced thin
 1 stalk celery, sliced thin
1½ pounds wild boar, *or* lean, dark pork, cubed
 ½ cup myrtle liqueur *or* ⅓ cup dry red wine and 2
   tablespoons raspberry liqueur
 1 tablespoon fresh rosemary leaves
 1 quart beef stock

salt and pepper to taste
2 potatoes, peeled and quartered lengthwise

In a soup pot, heat 1 tablespoon of the oil, then add the garlic, onion, carrot, and celery. Sauté for 5 minutes.

Scoop the vegetables out of the pot and reserve. Heat 2 more tablespoons of the oil in the same pot and brown the meat over high heat.

Pour in the liqueur or wine and allow it to reduce for 2 minutes. Add back the vegetables, then add the rosemary, stock, salt, and pepper.

Bring to a boil, reduce to a simmer, cover, and cook for 1 hour, or until the meat is tender.

In the meantime, boil the potatoes until just tender. Drain and refrigerate. Just before serving the stew, heat the last 2 tablespoons of oil and brown the potatoes on all sides until crispy.

Serve the stew in bowls with several pieces of potato on each serving.

Serves 2 to 3.

Malta

Malta is a tiny country lying about 60 miles south of Sicily. It consists of two treeless, limestone islands that have, over the millennia, like so much of the Mediterranean, played host to the Phoenicians, Greeks, Romans, Arabs, Normans, French, Italians, and finally the British. Malta's strategic location and good harbors have traditionally made it attractive to invaders.

The Maltese have their own language and their own culinary traditions, although both are a strong reflection of their history of invasions and occupations.

Their cuisine has been ingeniously assembled from what they have. Low rainfall and poor soil mean that their main crops are onions, potatoes, grains, figs, grapes, and olives, with some tomatoes, peppers, artichokes, and other heat and sun-loving vegetables. They raise virtually no animals, and in the old days were dependent on rabbits, small birds, and seafood, plus wild foods such as field herbs, honey, prickly pears, and capers.

Many soups in the Maltese cuisine require a long, slow, simmering time. This hearkens back to the days when it was impractical in tiny, crowded Malta for each home to have its own stove. Only open hearths were available, and a large pot with all the ingredients was pushed close to the heat to be left on its own for hours to slow cook. To this day, housewives in some small villages still bring their meals that require oven cooking to public bakeries to be done.

Traditionally, the Maltese eat very little meat; thus, their cuisine is heavy with simple vegetable and legume soups, with an egg or bit of cheese added for protein.

Maltese Vegetable Soup

        1 cup dried fava beans, soaked overnight
        2 tablespoons olive oil
        2 cloves garlic, minced
        2 onions, chopped
        1 head cabbage, cut into 8 pieces
        2 sprigs fresh thyme
    1½ quarts chicken stock
        3 potatoes, peeled and cubed
          salt and pepper to taste
        6 eggs
        6 Maltese *gbejniet,* *or* 6 heaping tablespoons ricotta
          cheese

Drain the fava beans. Cover again with fresh water, bring to a boil, and cook until they begin to get tender. Drain and reserve.

In a soup pot, heat the oil and lightly sauté the garlic and onions.

Add the cabbage, thyme, and reserved fava beans.

Pour in the stock, bring to a boil, reduce to a simmer, cover, and cook for 30 minutes.

Add the potatoes, salt, and pepper, and cook for another 30 minutes, or until all vegetables are tender.

Crack each egg into a shallow bowl, and slip each one carefully into the simmering soup. Or if it's easier, poach the eggs in a wide skillet of simmering, salted water.

When the eggs are done, divide the soup into 6 soup bowls, placing an egg in each one.

Top each serving with the ricotta-like little rounds of *gbejniet* cheese, or substitute a heaping tablespoon of ricotta for each serving.

Serves 6.

This recipe, from a Maltese-American friend, Lisa Gatt, is exactly as she gave it to me. Lisa says, "One of the most traditional and frequently cooked soups in Malta is *brodu*. In Malta this soup is often served as a main meal. It is generally cooked year round, but more frequently during the winter months. Although this soup has certain basic ingredients, the Maltese make it in a variety of ways."

"Brodu can be made using either beef, chicken, or turkey. The cooked meat is served as a side dish with the soup. The basics vegetables that are always used in brodu are onion, celery, and carrots, but other vegetables such as potatoes, zucchini, and kohlrabi are sometimes added. When this soup is being made with beef, a small amount of tomato paste is added for color as well as taste."

"Traditionally my family has brodu about once every two weeks, but mostly during the winter months. It is also my family's choice of soup for Thanksgiving and Christmas dinner. Chicken base is most preferred, but brodus made with beef, as well as the combination of two types of meat, are also enjoyed. The following recipe is my family's favorite variation of this soup."

Maltese Chicken Soup (Brodu Tat-Tigiega)

  1 whole chicken, about 3 pounds
  3 stalks celery, sliced
  4 carrots, peeled and sliced
  1 large onion, whole
    salt and pepper to taste
  2 small unpeeled zucchini, diced
  1/2 cup small pasta shapes, like orzo *or* 1/2 cup white rice *or*
    2 potatoes, peeled and diced

Clean and wash the chicken.

Place the chicken and its parts, such as gizzard, neck, and giblets in a large pot. Reserve the liver.

Cover with water and bring to a boil.

Add the celery, carrots, onion, salt, and pepper.

Lower to a simmer, cover, and cook for 2 1/2 hours. Carefully lift out the chicken and chicken parts.

Chop the liver and add it to the soup. Add the zucchini and pasta, rice, or potatoes. Cook for an additional 20 minutes.

Skim the fat off the finished soup. Serve the soup first, and the chicken separately.

Serves 4 to 6.

Vulcano

Off the northeast coast of Sicily lie the Aeolian Islands. Ferries and hydrofoils run a busy schedule, and for a few dollars you can pick one or all to visit. We had visited the top of volcanic Mount Etna in one of its calm periods, peering through the smoke and steam into its very heart. The Aeolian Islands are part of that same volcanic chain, and two, Vulcano and Stromboli, are always active.

Having seen the night-time fireworks of Stromboli before, we decided on the closer Vulcano, and made the thirteen-mile trip there by hydrofoil. We had heard that we would be going to an unusual place.

As the port came into view, we could see it was surrounded by dramatic, multi-colored cliffs. Sulfur, iron, and alum brightly stain the rock faces, but the surface of the hills, as well as the beach sand, is a deep lava black.

We walked back a block from the dock, and immediately encountered a bubbling mud lake. People were soaking in and smearing themselves with the therapeutic ooze. In the other direction a black hill, almost devoid of vegetation, had numerous steam vents, filling the air with sulfurous fumes.

The island is so small that we could walk across it in minutes, and after ascertaining that there had not been an eruption for 100 years, we found a cottage for rent on the far side. The beach there also had black sand. The water was clear and, not surprisingly, very warm.

Later we hired a boat with three other people, which took us around the island and into a dramatic water cave. The colorful cliffs, steam vents, and sulfurous smells were everywhere.

That evening, back on the pier, we had a fish soup typical of the small Italian islands, really a complete meal for two. It was its freshness and simplicity that sticks in our memory. Try to find an interesting assortment of shellfish—mussels, tiny clams, or anything else that your local fisherman or fishmonger may have that day.

Shellfish Stew à la Vulcano

      4 tablespoons olive oil
      6 cloves garlic
      1 onion, chopped
      1 carrot, peeled and chopped
      1 stalk celery, chopped
      1 cup dry white wine
      1 large tomato, peeled, seeded, and diced
    1/2 cup fresh parsley, chopped
    1/4 teaspoon hot red pepper flakes
      1 cup bottled clam juice
      1 cup chicken stock
      4 thick slices country-style bread
      4 dozen assorted shellfish, cleaned
        salt and pepper to taste

In a soup pot, heat 2 tablespoons of the oil. Mince 4 cloves of the garlic and sauté it, plus the onion, carrot, and celery for 5 minutes.

Pour the wine into the pot and allow it to boil and reduce by half.

Add the tomato, parsley, hot pepper, clam juice, and stock. Bring to a boil, reduce to a simmer, cover, and cook for 20 minutes.

In the meantime, brush the bread slices on both sides with the remaining 2 tablespoons of oil. Grill both sides under a broiler until slightly browned. Then rub each side with the 2 reserved garlic cloves.

Put all the shellfish into the soup. Raise the heat and toss the shellfish with a heavy spoon. Cover, then cook over medium heat for 6 minutes. Discard any shellfish that have failed to open. Add salt and pepper to taste.

Place one piece of garlic bread in each of 4 bowls. Divide the shellfish and spoon the soup over all. Serve immediately.

Serves 4.

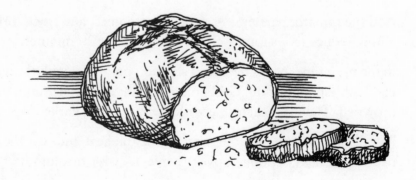

Paros

Everyone who visits Greece falls in love with her islands. They are too many to count, ranging from tiny uninhabited ones to giant Crete. We have been to a few—the justifiably well known Mykonos, with its picturesque main town and harbor, majestic Santorini (Thera), which is certainly one of the most beautiful islands in Greece if not the world, historic Delos, the sacred island of the ancients—but Paros continues to hold a special place in our hearts. It is quietly and quintessentially Greek. Staying in the town of Naoussa, we rented a wreck of a car and toured the island for several days one October.

Greek islands are a photographer's paradise, with their stark, barren landscapes, cycladic-style villages, white churches, blue skies, and beautiful people. On Paros, we drove and hiked everywhere, taking hundreds of pictures.

Each night we returned to Naoussa and its pretty harbor, to enjoy the sunset and watch the fishermen bringing in their catch and the old women gossiping in its tiny square. Several plain, outdoor restaurants line the dock, ready to receive the freshest fish. We watched as the fishermen kneaded and slapped octopus against the stone pier, using an ancient method to tenderize them. They looked like laundry being pounded clean and hung out to rest on wires that stretched overhead.

Large and small fish, along with several varieties of shellfish, filled circular wire baskets being unloaded from small wooden fishing boats. This same scene was, we felt sure, being repeated that evening in hundreds of similar villages throughout the islands. After all, "Greek" and "fishermen" are practically synonymous.

A classic soup of the Greek Islands, which we enjoyed on both nights in Naoussa, is called *kakavia*. It is similar to bouillabaisse and is of the same origin. Both are country soups which depend on the availability of a variety of fresh fish. In both cases, fishermen gather up any unsold fish and bring them home to be cooked up with oil, garlic, tomatoes, and other good things to feed their families.

Kakavia

3 tablespoons olive oil
3 cloves garlic, minced
2 large onions, sliced thin
2 stalks celery, sliced into 1/2-inch pieces
2 leeks, white parts only, cleaned and sliced
2 carrots, peeled and sliced into 1/2-inch pieces
1 cup dry white wine
    juice of 1 lemon
2 14-ounce cans diced tomatoes
3 bay leaves
2 sprigs fresh thyme
    salt and pepper to taste
3 pounds assorted, cleaned, and boned fish, cut in large
    chunks (snapper, flounder, bass, monkfish, etc.)
3 dozen assorted, cleaned, shellfish (clams, mussels,
    shrimp, calamari,* *and/or* small lobster tails)
3 cups water (more or less)

In a deep soup pot, heat the oil, and slowly sauté the garlic, onion, celery, leeks, and carrots. They should not brown. Sauté for 8 minutes.

Pour in the wine and allow it to boil for another 3 minutes.

Add the lemon juice, tomatoes, bay leaves, thyme, salt, and pepper. Bring to a boil, lower to a simmer, and cook for 30 minutes.

Begin to add the fish and shellfish. Start with the biggest pieces and longest cooking items. Some especially thick pieces of fish take up to

10 minutes. Lobster tails take about 8 minutes. Clams and mussels needed to cook for 6 minutes (discard any that do not open). Shrimp take only 3 minutes, calamari slices about 2 minutes. Add enough water to cover but no more. Simmer, but do not boil.

Unlike bouillabaisse, Greek fish soups are served, soup and fish together, in deep bowls with lots of crusty bread on the side.

Serves 6 to 8.

Note: See page 37 about how to clean calamari.

Cyprus

If meats are used at all in Mediterranean soups, it is pork, chicken, and lamb that predominate. Pork would never be used, of course, in Muslim North Africa, Turkey, or the Middle East, but on Cyprus it is used to make a delicious pork and onion stew called *afelia*. It is served with lots of bread, rather than over rice or pasta.

Pork and Onion Stew (Afelia)

1 1/2 pounds lean pork, cut in 1-inch cubes
4 tablespoons olive oil
salt and freshly ground black pepper to taste
1 tablespoon coriander seeds *or* ground coriander
5 onions, sliced thin
1 cup red wine
2 cups beef stock
1/2 cup fresh parsley, minced
1/4 cup fresh cilantro *or* 1 tablespoon fresh rosemary, minced

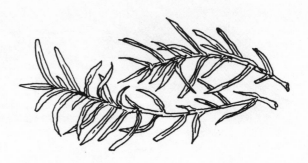

Toss the pork cubes with a bit of the oil to coat. Then salt and pepper the cubes. Grind the coriander seeds fine and put them (or the ground coriander) on the pork. Rub all the seasonings into the meat. Allow it to sit for 1 hour.

In the meantime, slowly sauté the onions in 2 tablespoons of the oil. Set aside.

After an hour, heat all the remaining oil very hot and quickly sauté the pork cubes until they brown.

Pour in the wine, then let it boil over high heat to reduce it by half. Then pour in the stock and the reserved onions, plus the parsley. Reduce the heat, cover, and let it cook for 45 minutes, or until the pork is tender.

Add the cilantro or rosemary. Let it simmer for another 10 minutes. Serve hot.

Serves 4.

Courtyard, Mykonos, Greece

Auxiliary Recipes—
"The Extras"

Use these traditional sauces, croutons, and condiments to begin or finish many of the soups in this book.

But don't stop at soups; with your imagination and some of my suggestions, use them as marinades, spreads, and sauces over meats, fish, and vegetables.

This North African sauce and marinade is used in several soups, including Egyptian Molokhia Soup. Also use it to finish vegetables and fish, and as a marinade for chicken, fish, and lamb.

Tekliyah Sauce

    4 cloves garlic, chopped
    1/2 cup packed fresh cilantro
    1/2 teaspoon ground cumin
    1/4 teaspoon or more, cayenne pepper
    1/2 cup olive oil
       salt to taste

Put all the ingredients in a blender and process until smooth. Do not over process. Keeps refrigerated for up to 5 days.

As to the preparation of kibbeh, I'd like to use the exact words of a Lebanese-American friend, Bob Zogby. Here is his description of his grandmother's method:

"Kibbeh is the national dish of Syria and Lebanon. The secret is to pound the mixture so well that it forms a paste. It is a laborious feat to achieve the desired texture and taste. My grandmother (*sitto* in Arabic) used to be a master at this, with her 'blessed hands,' until her arthritis began. The traditional method is simple, but its achievement requires 'indefatigable hands.' To save time and energy, a meat grinder, using a fine blade, will suffice, but it loses the flavor of the old fashioned 'grinding and kneading.'"

Buy the bulgur in a Middle Eastern grocer and use this kibbeh as directed in designated soups.

Kibbeh

> 2 cups fine bulgur, also called burghul or cracked wheat
> 2 pounds very lean leg of lamb, ground twice on the finest blade
> 1 large onion, grated (catch the juice, too)
> 1½ teaspoons salt
> ½ teaspoon pepper
> ¼ teaspoon ground allspice

Soak the bulger for 10 minutes in cold water. Drain and squeeze dry in cheesecloth.

Combine bulger, lamb, onion, salt, pepper, and allspice in a bowl.

Knead for 15 to 20 minutes until very smooth.* Add a little water to your hands or the mixture, if necessary. Proceed as directed in the soup recipes. Freezes well.

Note: I use my food processor on pulse for a few seconds to short-cut this step; we won't tell "sitto."

Pistou, the sauce traditionally added to French "minestrone" or bean and vegetable soup, has been described as pesto without the nuts. Try it as a quick sauce over pasta. This recipe comes from Valérie Morvan, who grew up in Marseilles.

Pistou

    4 cloves garlic, chopped
    1 ripe tomato, peeled, seeded, and diced
    1 cup fresh basil leaves, packed
    2/3 cup grated cheese, such as Parmesan
      salt and pepper to taste
    2/3 cup olive oil

Put the garlic, tomato, basil, cheese, salt, and pepper in a blender and purée. With the blender going, slowly add the oil, until the mixture thickens somewhat. Do not over-process.

Pistou will keep up to 5 days in the refrigerator.

The traditional finish for bourride, *aioli* is a garlic mayonnaise, equally at home on poached fish and sandwiches.

Aioli

    3 cloves garlic, chopped
    1/4 teaspoon salt, or to taste
    2 egg yolks
    1 tablespoon fresh lemon juice *or* vinegar
    1/2 cup canola oil, plus 1/2 cup olive oil, mixed

Place the garlic, salt, egg yolks, and lemon or vinegar in a blender and purée.

Slowly add the mixed oils, with the blender running, until a mayonnaise forms. You may not need to use all the oil. Do not over-process.

Refrigerate and use within 2 days.

This sauce is a classic finish for bouillabaisse and a delicious final addition to fish dishes and vegetables.

Rouille

              1 cup fresh bread pieces, no crusts
            1/2 cup chicken stock or water
              4 cloves garlic, chopped
            1/2 teaspoon saffron, soaked in 1 tablespoon water for 10
                minutes
              2 egg yolks
         1 or 2 hot red peppers
            1/8 teaspoon salt, or to taste
            1/2 cup olive oil

Soak the bread in the stock or water for 5 minutes. Squeeze out any excess.

Put the bread, garlic, saffron, and egg yolks in a food processor or blender.

Take the core and seeds out of the peppers and cut the flesh into pieces. Place the peppers and salt into the blender.

Turn on the blender and purée the ingredients. Slowly add the oil while the blender is running, until a mayonnaise forms. Do not over-process.

Refrigerate and use within 2 days.

Greek avgolemono sauce is used, not only as the last ingredient added to many of their soups, but also by itself over steamed vegetables, meat, and fish. This recipe is the standard one for the plain sauce. Although it is fine as is, to add to soups, make it the way it is described in each soup recipe.

Avgolemono Sauce

  2 eggs
  4 tablespoons lemon juice (1 lemon)
  1/2 cup chicken stock
    salt and pepper to taste

Beat the eggs well. Pour into a small saucepan with the lemon juice, stock, salt, and pepper. Slowly raise the heat and whisk constantly until the sauce thickens. Do not allow it to boil.

Use immediately or refrigerate for up to 2 days. Reheat gently in a double boiler when ready to serve.

Little bits of preserved lemon peel are used in soups and other foods in North Africa. They have a lovely scent and unique taste. Although grated lemon peel can be substituted, the flavor of these is much more intense.

Preserved Lemons

16 lemons, divided
1 cup fresh lemon juice
1/2 cup kosher salt
1 tablespoon cardamon pods, cracked
3 cinnamon sticks
4 bay leaves

Squeeze the juice from enough of the lemons to make about 1 cup. Set aside.

You should have at least 8 unblemished lemons left. Cut them in quarters from the top to within 1/2-inch of the bottom. Leave the 4 sections attached, but slightly spread the quarters apart.

In the bottom of a clean glass jar with a tightly fitting lid, put 1 tablespoon of the salt. Put in the lemons, remaining salt, and spices in alternating layers. Push down on the lemons to make them fit.

Pour in the lemon juice. Add more juice if needed to cover the lemons and spices. Leave a little space at the top. Screw on the lid.

Put the jar in the refrigerator, and shake once a day for 3 weeks.

To use the lemons: After 3 weeks open the jar, and pull off one section of a lemon. Rinse and dry. Trim off the pulp and discard. Thinly slice or chop the peel and use as needed for a recipe.

Unused lemons will keep refrigerated for 1 year.

There are many recipes for this fiery red condiment most often associated with North African cuisine. Here are two of them. Feel free to make them even hotter!

Harissa I

> 1 tablespoon lime juice
> 2 tablespoons olive oil
> 2 tablespoons tomato paste
> 1 teaspoon ground cumin
> 1/2 teaspoon coriander
> 1 teaspoon or more ground cayenne pepper
> 1/4 teaspoon salt

Whisk together all the ingredients, or put them in a small blender and purée. Harissa will keep well refrigerated for several weeks.

Harissa II

> 2 tablespoons sun-dried tomatoes
> 3 tablespoons or more dried hot red pepper flakes
> 2 garlic cloves, chopped
> 1/8 teaspoon salt
> 1/4 cup olive oil

Place the tomatoes and pepper flakes in 2 small bowls. Pour a little boiling water over each, then soak them for 20 minutes.

Strain the liquid carefully from each.

Place the tomatoes, pepper flakes, garlic, salt, and olive oil in a small blender. Purée until all is a smooth paste.

Harissa will keep well refrigerated for several weeks.

Garlic Bread

> 1-inch thick slices country-style Italian bread (1 or more for each serving of soup)
> 2 to 4 tablespoons olive oil
> 2 or more large garlic cloves, peeled
> salt and pepper to taste (optional)

Brush each slice of bread on both sides with the oil.

Brown them; first one side, then the other, under a broiler.

Immediately rub both sides of each piece of crisp bread with the garlic cloves.

If you wish, sprinkle lightly with salt and pepper. Used immediately, either in a soup or served separately.

Croutons

> 5 1/2-inch thick slices country-style Italian bread
> 2 tablespoons olive oil
>   salt to taste

You can either remove the bread crusts or not. Then, brush the slices lightly with oil. Cut into 1/2-inch cubes. Sprinkle with salt.

Spread the cubes on a baking sheet, and bake in a 350° oven until they are crisp and dry, about 10 minutes. Use immediately.

Garlic Croutons

> 1/2 cup olive oil
>   5 cloves garlic, sliced
>   5 1/2-inch thick slices country-style Italian bread
>   salt to taste

In a skillet, heat the oil and slowly sauté the garlic until slightly browned. Remove the garlic from the oil and discard.

Cut the bread into 1/2-inch cubes. Sauté them in the hot oil until they brown. Add salt.

Scoop them out and drain on paper towels. Serve immediately.

Use this basic recipe, or good quality bottled clam broth, in all fish soup recipes. In many of these recipes chicken stock is called for, but feel free to substitute this stock to get a more full fish flavor.

Fish Stock

>   2 pounds fish and bones from fresh non-oily fish such as
>   snapper, sole, or grouper
>   1 cup dry white wine
>   1 carrot, peeled and coarsely chopped
>   1 onion, quartered
>   1/2 cup fresh parsley
>   1 bay leaf
>   salt and pepper to taste

Remove all traces of blood, gills, fat, skin, fins, and tail.

Put the flesh and bones in a pot and add water to cover. Add the wine, carrot, onion, parsley, bay leaf, salt, and pepper. Bring it to a boil, reduce to a simmer, cover, and cook for 35 minutes.

Strain, then discard the vegetables, flesh, and bones.

Cover the stock and refrigerate for up to 2 days. Stock may be frozen for up to 1 month.

Use this basic recipe, or good quality canned chicken stock, in all recipes calling for it.

Chicken Stock

> 3 pounds chicken necks, backs, wings, and/or gizzards
> 2¹/2 quarts water
> 2 stalks celery with leaves, coarsely chopped
> 2 carrots, peeled and coarsely chopped
> 1 onion, quartered
> 2 bay leaves
> 2 sprigs parsley (see note)
> ¹/2 teaspoon whole peppercorns
> salt to taste

In a soup pot, combine all the ingredients.

Bring it to a boil, reduce to a simmer, cover, and cook for 2 to 3 hours.

Strain, then save the chicken, bones, and vegetables for another use, or discard.

Pour the strained stock into clean containers, cover, and refrigerate for up to 2 days.

When chilled, skim off and discard any fat that has congealed on the surface. Stock may be frozen for up to 2 months.

Note: For chicken stock intended for use in Middle Eastern, Greek, or North African recipes, you may wish to add small amounts of dill, thyme, mint, or basil to taste.

Soups in this book that contain lamb designate canned chicken or beef stock because canned lamb stock is not available. However, if you can and do make this lamb stock, substitute it for the chicken or beef stocks in lamb soups.

Lamb Stock

      3 pounds meaty lamb bones
      2 quarts water
      1 onion, quartered
      1 carrot, peeled and coarsely chopped
    2/3 cup fresh parsley
      1 bay leaf
      1 sprig fresh thyme
        salt to taste
    1/2 teaspoon whole peppercorns

Place the bones on a baking sheet and roast them in a 350° oven for 1 1/2 to 2 hours.

In a soup pot, combine all the ingredients. Bring it to a boil, reduce to a simmer, cover, and cook for 2 to 3 hours.

Strain, then save the bones and vegetables for another use, or discard.

Pour the strained stock into clean containers, cover, and refrigerate for up to 2 days. When cold, skim off and discard any fat that has congealed on the surface.

Stock may be frozen for up to 2 months.

Use this basic recipe, or good quality canned beef stock, in all recipes calling for it.

Beef Stock

> 3 pounds meaty beef bones
> 2 quarts water
> 1 onion, quartered
> 1 clove garlic, sliced
> 2 stalks celery with leaves, coarsely chopped
> 2 carrots, peeled and coarsely chopped
> 2 bay leaves
> 2 sprigs parsley
>   salt to taste
> 1/2 teaspoon whole peppercorns

Place the bones on a baking sheet, and roast them in a 350° oven for about 1 1/2 to 2 hours.

In a soup pot, combine all the ingredients. Bring it to a boil, reduce to a simmer, cover, and cook for 2 to 3 hours.

Strain, then save the beef bones and vegetables for another use, or discard.

Pour the strained stock into clean containers, cover, and refrigerate for up to 2 days.

When cold, skim off and discard any fat that has congealed on the surface.

Stock may be frozen for up to 2 months.

Doorway, Eze, France

Index

Carol and David Robertson have traveled extensively in Europe, Asia, and Africa, both professionally and for pleasure. Carol is an artist and teacher, and David is a retired professor of photography from Rochester Institute of Technology in Rochester, New York. They now make their home in Juno Beach, Florida.

Their previous collaborations include *Portuguese Cooking: The Authentic and Robust Cuisine of Portugal* (North Atlantic Books), *Turkish Cooking: A Culinary Journey Through Turkey* (Frog, Ltd.), and *Vegetarian Turkish Cooking: Over 100 of Turkey's Classic Recipes for the Vegetarian Cook* (Frog, Ltd.).